# WRITING THE NEW ECONOMY

JOHN MIDDLETON

WRITING THE NEW ECONOMY

THE ULTIMATE E-BUSINESS LIBRARY

CAPSTONE

First published 2000 by
Capstone Publishing, Inc.          Capstone Publishing Limited
40 Commerce Park                   8 Newtec Place
Milford                            Oxford OX4 1RE
CT 06460                           United Kingdom
USA                                http://www.capstone.co.uk
Contact: info@capstonepub.com

CIP catalogue records for this book are available from the British Library
and the US Library of Congress
US Library of Congress Card Number: 00-108014

ISBN 1-84112-106-1

Typeset in 10.5/13 pt Plantin by
Sparks Computer Solutions Ltd, Oxford, UK
http://www.sparks.co.uk
Printed and bound by
TJ International Ltd, Padstow, Cornwall

This book is printed on acid-free paper

Substantial discounts on bulk quantities of Capstone books are available to
corporations, professional associations and other organizations. If you are in the
USA or Canada, phone the LPC Group, Special Sales Department for details on
(1-800-626-4330) or fax (1-800-334-3892). Everywhere else, phone Capstone
Publishing on (+44-1865-798623) or fax (+44-1865-240941).

"When old words die out on the tongue,
new melodies break forth from the heart;
and where the old tracks are lost,
new country is revealed with its wonders."

*Rabindranath Tagore*

# Contents

# *Acknowledgements*

I'd like to thank:

- Mark Allin at Capstone who showed that the skills of a top-class editor are like those of the very best waiters – hovering when needed, and nowhere to be seen when not.
- The "Friends of Capstone" – an unrivaled group of business brains whose advice, tips, and comments about which books should be featured here (and, just as crucially, which titles in their view didn't merit a place) helped me to end up with a final list that was a vast improvement over my initial attempt. The final decision though about what went in was mine, so I alone deserve it on the chin for any howlers, omissions, or glaring errors of judgment.
- All the writers and contributors to *Future Filter*, particularly Bob Gorzynski, Andrew Jones, Ann Rippin and June Burrough, whose regular pearls of wisdom have enhanced my understanding of the new economy and whose book reviews of some of the titles featured in *Writing the New Economy* have added intellectual ballast to my writing.

Finally, I could not have written this book without the support of my wife Julie, particularly during the final days of writing. Thanks also to our children Guy and Helena who, if they ever think about the new economy when they are grown up and working, will probably wonder what all the fuss was about. To you all with love.

# Introduction:
# Defining the New Economy

"Knowledge constantly makes itself obsolete, with the result that today's advance knowledge is tomorrow's ignorance."
Peter Drucker, writing in *Harvard Business Review*,
September–October 1997

"It's tough to predict – especially about the future."
Attributed to Sam Goldwyn

F or something that has spawned millions of words over the past 12 months alone, the "new economy" remains a curiously hazy term. The phrase has no obvious inventor, no single point of origin. Journals and newspapers like the *Economist* or the *Financial Times* are agreed that dot.com companies operate in the "new economy," but beyond that, the phrase is a bit like the inkblots in the Rorschach test – people seem to project their own meaning onto the words.

This book argues that the tendrils of the new economy stretch wide and deep. The new information technologies that have brought dot.com businesses into being are simultaneously restructuring global markets and whole industry sectors, challenging conventional economic thinking, redefining how business is done, and impacting to varying degrees on every worker in the global marketplace.

Reflecting this, *Writing the New Economy* explores a wispy combination of inter-connected phenomena that embrace, *inter alia*, globalization, the transformative impact of technology on organizational life (indeed on the very nature of organizations), successful e-business models, and the changing nature of working life for us individually.

Each of the 50 books highlighted in *Writing the New Economy* contributes its own distinctive piece to the jigsaw. From the overall picture, however, ten clear themes emerge:

## 1 Growing pains, not death throes

In June 2000, Lehman Brothers published a report suggesting that Amazon, the biggest and – according to many – the best of the e-tailers, could go broke within a year. This report, sandwiched as it was between the high-profile crashes of boo.com in May 2000 and Clickmango two months later, contributed to a slump in dot.com share prices, and caused a number of commentators to gleefully predict the death of e-commerce. A more positive (and convincing) interpretation is that the heady optimism which accompanied stock-market flotations like lastminute.com's in the early months of 2000 has given way to a more sensible and grounded reappraisal of Internet businesses.

The Internet's period of grace may be over but its future seems assured. The number of web users is climbing steeply, and this growth spurt is set to continue. Another positive indicator is that there are now well over 15 million registered domain names worldwide (of which just over one million have been registered in the UK).

For companies, the electronic market place is opening up a wealth of new opportunities. By enabling the creation of a global marketplace, and by decentralizing control and empowering people all along the information chain, technology redefines what is possible for organizations and customers alike.

The new economy is here to stay, and participation in it is becoming a pre-requisite for corporate survival. As Andy Grove, President and CEO of Intel, puts it, "Within five years all companies will be Internet companies or they won't be companies at all. In other words, companies not using the Internet to improve just about every facet of their business operation will be destroyed by competitors who do."

## 2 The new economy is a work-in-progress

Eric Hobsbawm expresses this well:

> "We are certainly a single global economy compared with thirty years ago, but we can say with equal certainty that we'll be even more globalized in 2050, and very much more in 2100.

Globalization is not the product of a single action, like switching on a light or starting a car engine. It is a historical process that has undoubtedly speeded up enormously in the last ten years, but it is a permanent, constant transformation. It is not at all clear, therefore, at what stage we can say it has reached its final destination and can be considered complete. This is principally because it essentially involves expanding across a globe that is by its very nature varied geographically, climatically, and historically. This reality imposes certain limitations on the unification of the entire planet. However, we are all agreed that globalization, and especially the globalized economy, has made such spectacular progress that today you couldn't talk of an international division of labor as we did before the seventies."

## 3  *The new economy redefines traditional economic principles ...*

Much economic theory, for example, is still based on the scarcity axiom. But consider the fax machine, says Kevin Kelly: when the first fax rolled off the conveyor belt around 1965, "it was worth nothing. Zero. The second fax machine to be made immediately made the first one worth something. There was someone to fax to. Because fax machines are linked into a network, each additional fax machine that is shipped increases the value of all the fax machines operating before it." To use a Kellyism, plentitude, not scarcity, generates value.

## *... except where it doesn't*

Even for dot.coms, profits still matter. These days, they need to show the stock markets that, with every quarter, they are getting closer to making money. To satisfy potential investors, those dot.coms now going public typically need to convince that they can be in the black within a couple of years at most.

## 4  *The new economy favours intangibles*

When it comes to achieving business success, the traditional factors of production – land, labour and capital – are rapidly becoming restraints rather than driving forces. Knowledge has become the central, key resource. Nicholas Negroponte writes about the shift of emphasis from atoms to bits. Ideas and information are the currency of the new economy, not the stuff you can drop on your toe.

## 5 The new economy supplements the traditional economy; it does not supplant it

As Kevin Kelly has put it, "the old economies will continue to operate profitably within the deep cortex of the new economy." The fact is that around the world there are just as many cars and ships being constructed as ever, just as many roads being built, just as much coal being produced, as much steel being made. Eric Hobsbawm writes that it is a mistake to talk of a post-industrial era, because in reality those goods and services that were produced in the industrial era are still being produced today. The difference is where they are now being produced. Although in the UK Indian restaurants may employ more people than the steel, coal mining and ship building industries combined (*The Times*, 18 May 2000), "traditional" industries are all thriving elsewhere in the world.

## 6 Size doesn't matter

In *The Death of Distance*, Frances Cairncross describes how, by using technology creatively, small companies can now offer services that, in the past, only giants could provide. What's more, the cost of starting new businesses is declining, and so more small companies will spring up. Many companies will become networks of independent specialists; more employees will therefore work in smaller units or alone.

Individuals with valuable ideas can attract global venture capital. Perhaps one of the most telling features of the new economy is that increasing numbers of people can describe themselves without irony as one-person global businesses.

## 7 The local labour exchange has become a global job market

Manufacturing capacity will continue to shift from Western economies to those countries with access to cheaper labour. Equally, technology is allowing more and more knowledge-based work to be shipped to the cheapest environment. This may bring jobs to emerging economies but can create severe pressures for unskilled workers in more advanced economies.

## 8 Blue collars were the first to feel the pinch; white collars will be next

The loss of many jobs to wholly automated systems is changing the white-collar workplace to the same degree that it has already transformed the factory floor. Tom Peters predicts that 90% of white-collar jobs in the US will either be destroyed or altered beyond recognition in the next 10 to 15 years. As he puts it, "That's a catastrophic prediction, given that 90% of us are engaged in white-collar work of one sort or another."

## 9 24/7 is the new 9–5

The "working day" has no meaning in a global village where communication via electronic mail, voice mail, and facsimile transmissions can be sent or received at any time of day or night.

## 10 Bad news: nobody owes you a career

According to Michael Dunkerley, "People are now becoming the most expensive optional component of the productive process and technology is becoming the cheapest."

As companies gain more technological savvy, they become less tied to time or place, and less reliant on a large, permanent workforce. Against this backdrop, the notion of lifetime employment in one company has all but disappeared.

The consequence of this, says Andy Grove, is that "your career is literally your business. You own it as a sole proprietor. You have one employee: yourself. You are in competition with millions of similar businesses: millions of other employees all over the world. You need to accept ownership of your career, your skills and the timing of your moves. It is your responsibility to protect this personal business of yours from harm and to position it to benefit from the changes in the environment. Nobody else can do that for you."

## Sources

Frances Cairncross (1997) *The Death of Distance*, Orion Publishing, UK.

Peter Drucker (1993) interview in *Wired* magazine, July.

Michael Dunkerley (1996) *The Jobless Economy*, Blackwell, USA.

Andrew S. Grove (1996) *Only the Paranoid Survive*, HarperCollinsBusiness, USA.

Eric Hobsbawm (2000) *The New Century*, Little, Brown and Company, UK.

Kevin Kelly (1998) *New Rules for the New Economy*, Fourth Estate, UK.

Nicholas Negroponte (1995) *Being Digital*, Knopf, USA.

Tom Peters (2000) in an article entitled "What will we do for work?", *Time* magazine, 29 May.

## *About* Writing the New Economy

At the heart of *Writing the New Economy* are reviews of 50 key books that explore various facets of the new economy. The key ideas in each book are summarized and assessed. For ease of reference, the books featured are presented in alphabetical order by author.

In addition, there is an extensive annotated bibliography at the back of the book, as well as a glossary of key new economy terms, and a guide to further sources of information for those wishing to delve deeper.

In the absence of a single, definitive text about the new economy, and reflecting a maxim of Tom Petzinger's that "nobody's as smart as everybody," it may well be that *Writing the New Economy* represents the most comprehensive overview of the new economy currently available in book form.

## A cautionary note

> "In the industrial age, information was like gold. In the digital age, it is like milk – use it quickly."
> Source: Consultancy NUA's advertising slogan

In terms of speed and depth of impact, our planet has never experienced anything quite like the Internet. Other great transformative technologies – railways, electricity, the telephone, the motor car, and so on – took decades to achieve the kind of critical mass that the Internet has attained in a handful of years.

This unprecedented speed of change, coupled with the rate at which our knowledge of the new economy and our understanding of what does and doesn't work in this new business environment is growing, has made the task of selecting the 50 "best" books on the new economy a tad daunting. All too often, books hailed on publication as groundbreaking have within a couple of years been fully absorbed into the e-business bloodstream, their once stunning insights reduced to the status of the blindingly obvious.

This has been particularly evident with books that focus on the technology of the new economy. There have been some excellent books, but most have dated very rapidly.

In selecting books for inclusion, every effort has been made to pick out books that have something practical to offer businesses over the next few years. That said, there will inevitably be one or two books featured in *Writing the New Economy* whose impact will be short-lived. It is equally inevitable that there will be new books appearing in the weeks and months ahead that merit inclusion. These issues will be addressed by the publication in due course of a second edition.

In the meantime, here are 50 books whose common feature is that they all challenge our thinking about and inform our understanding of the new economy. For me, reading and re-reading these books hammers home the exhilarating truth of a line from Tom Stoppard's play *Arcadia:* "It's the best possible time to be alive, when almost everything you thought you knew is wrong."

*John Middleton*
*Bristol, England*
*September 2000*

# Fifty Books that Define the New Economy

# ROBERT BALDOCK

# *The Last Days of the Giants?*

## 2000

"S ize does matter" proclaimed posters advertising the 1998 movie *Godzilla*. And certainly the latest wave of mergers, acquisitions, and strategic alliances seem to tell us that the future belongs to the corporate giants. On the other hand, the view that big is beautiful has looked less and less convincing in recent times as we see corporate giants being consistently upstaged and outthought by smaller, nimbler rivals.

Robert Baldock sees major problems ahead for any of us working in those organizations that have come to believe that their sheer size will protect them from the unpredictability of the next few years. "The environment in which the culture of 'bigness' blossomed is fast disappearing in many industries," he tells us.

However, the question mark in the title of Baldock's book is significant – the corporate giants of late 20th century may be in serious trouble but he believes they can survive in the intensely competitive environment of the 21st if they radically alter the way they do things. He highlights three areas in particular where the giants may need to change their outlook. These are:

1  *The nature of what they offer to their customers.* Most companies have traditionally sold products or services to their customers. Increasingly companies will need to think in terms of selling solutions and, beyond that, of satisfying customer intentions. An intention, explains Baldock, is "a desire or goal that may take a person many years to achieve and may involve the integration of products and solutions from multiple firms spanning many industries. For example, 'Having an enjoyable retirement' could involve a move to a sunny climate, a new hobby, making financial provisions for your

nearest and dearest, and so on." The further a company can move away from simply selling products and services towards providing solutions and satisfying intentions, the better it will be able to differentiate its offerings from the competition's.

2   *The nature of the relationship they have with their customers.* Is the business seller-driven, customer centric, or buyer driven? Historically, large organizations have presumed to know what the market might want to buy. More recently, the world has become more customer-centric with sellers trying to tailor their offerings to meet fast-changing consumer needs. Baldock predicts that "we are entering a buyer driven era, an era in which the customer will not just be a king, but a dictator." More than just an extreme form of the customer-centric model, Baldock suggests that in a buyer driven world, sellers may not have direct contact with consumers but might have to deal with a trusted intermediary selected by the consumer. These intermediaries will in effect invite selected sellers to bid for the business. There is no room in such a market for producers to draw any conclusions in advance about what customers might want.

3   *Their level of virtualization.* At the first level, the company tries to do everything in-house. At the second, the company selectively outsources work to third parties. Beyond the outsourcing model lies the virtual enterprise, carrying very few processes itself and concentrating its efforts of organizing the efforts of others. Baldock defines virtualization as "the removal of constraints of form, place and time made possible by the convergence of computing, communications and content."

Combining these three elements, the optimal 21st-century organization, says Baldock, will be a buyer-driven virtual enterprise that satisfies consumer intentions.

His prescription for big business survival involves three stages:

- first, companies should re-assess the economics of sales and delivery channels with a view to dumping excess baggage;
- second, they should move to a more customer-centric business model "where their pared-down products and distribution channels are integrated and closely aligned with the key buyer values of their customer segments"; and
- finally, they must turn their business model through 180 degrees in order to come up with value-creating packages that satisfy consumer intentions.

Whether Baldock truly has come up with a route map for big business survival is open to question, but *The Last Days of the Giants?* is necessary bedtime reading for any large company CEO whose business is in danger of being taken to the cleaners by upstart dot.com competitors.

## Reality check

Although Baldock believes that large companies can survive over the coming decades, he is realist enough to acknowledge that there are several forces that are working against industrial gigantism. Among the most significant are:

- The arrival of new, Internet-based firms that are more agile and innovative than the giants. The Internet is helping to put small agile newcomers on a par with large corporations and able to compete head on with them for new business. Just as Microsoft could appear from virtually nowhere to usurp the market of mighty IBM, so a few years later Netscape appeared overnight and threatened to undermine the market (and the size) of Microsoft. Who will be next? And where will they come from? In this world, small agile firms have an advantage over giant organizations that are unable to take decisions quickly. This process will accelerate as more and more companies join the e-commerce bandwagon.
- A shift in power from the seller to the buyer. The convergence of computing, communications and content in the shape of personal computers (PCs) hooked up over a network to the Internet has triggered a revolution in the way business is conducted. Users of these technologies have 24-hour access to almost everything, everywhere. Internet-based search agents make it possible for these users to track down the cheapest products in seconds, and new Internet-based intermediaries (the so-called 'Infomediaries') have created a new form of commerce whereby the buyer sets the price, not the seller.
- Changing government attitudes towards the giants. Governments have become less enchanted with big business. They have stopped mergers from going ahead and have sought to break up some of the larger firms to create more competition. Through a program of deregulation they have also forced the large incumbents to focus more on the needs of their customers and to drop their prices.

### Zeitbite

"Somewhere out there is a bullet with your company's name on it. Somewhere out there is a competitor, unborn and unknown, that will render your business model obsolete. Bill Gates knows that. When he says that Microsoft is always two years away from failure, he's not just blowing smoke ... The hottest and most dangerous new business models out there are on the Web."

Gary Hamel, *Fortune* magazine, 1998

- Industry convergence. Many large companies are moving into new markets (e.g. retailers into financial services). They are doing this for one of two reasons: either because their own markets give them little scope for growth; or as part of a drive to hang onto their most profitable customers by offering them a broader range of products and services. In both cases, these assaults on new markets are being made with new products or services at incredibly low prices.
- A very short-term focus. Institutional investors and brokers' analysts have become very demanding of public companies. In the United States in particular, they relentlessly demand an improvement in results every quarter. Fail to deliver against this expectation and top managers are out, regardless of their past track record. Against this backdrop, companies have become reluctant to make large, long-term investments for fear of damaging their short-term results.

These five forces have led to the most competitive environment in the history of commerce, and they spell big trouble for the giants that may have become too big to respond quickly to the threats that they pose.

Derived from *The Last Days of the Giants?*

## Is your company too big for its boots?

Baldock offers readers this simple test. If you can positively identify with any of the following statements:

- Current mergers and acquisitions activity will continue unabated well into the 21st century.
- Flashy Internet start-ups cannot threaten our core activities built up over years of careful planning, research, branding and marketing.
- Our sheer size will protect us from the unpredictability of the next few years.
- We will manage our customers; they will not manage us
- The government will always have the best interests of big business at heart.
- A long-term focus is the key to success
- We do not see the value of outsourcing
- Just because we are big, it doesn't mean we cannot move quickly

then you and your company may be in very serious trouble.

## The author

Robert Baldock is Chief Executive of @speed, an organization that aims to help people save time and improve their quality of life. He was previously a global managing partner with Andersen Consulting, who he joined in 1976 at the age of 21, before going on in 1987 to become one of the youngest people ever to make partner in the firm. In his spare time, he is Chairman of the UK Motorsport Industry Association, the trade body representing British motorsport.

*The Last Days of the Giants?* is his second book. His first – *Destination Z: the History of the Future* (Wiley, 1998) – looked at the future shape of consumer serving industries.

## Sources and further reading

Baldock, Robert (2000) *The Last Days of the Giants?* Wiley, UK.

# TIM BERNERS-LEE

## Weaving the Web

## 1999

T echnology has become such a part of our lives that we almost cease to notice it. When did you last wonder about how a light bulb works – a century or so ago, it would have been amazing. Similarly, most of us now take desktop computing for granted, and yet ENIAC, commonly thought of as the first modern computer, was built as recently as 1944.

Since then, the speed of technological advancement has been staggering, particularly in the field of computing technology. ENIAC weighed several tons, consumed 140,000 watts of electricity and could execute up to 5,000 basic arithmetic operations per second. In contrast, some of the latest PCs, weigh less than two pounds, use less than 2 watts of electricity, and can execute millions of instructions per second.

But in terms of extent and speed of impact, the Internet has outpaced all of the great disruptive technologies of the 20th century – electricity, the telephone, the motor car, and so on.

The Internet started life as ARPANET (Advanced Research Project Agency Network), a computer network that the US Department of Defense set up in 1969. The original aim was modest – to allow computer scientists and engineers working on military contracts all over America to share expensive computers and other resources. A key requirement for the network was for it to be able to continue to work even if some cables connecting these computers were destroyed. The solution was to develop a computer network that had no fixed center and no fixed routes. Each computer connects to a small number of neighbors, which in turn have a few different neighbors.

In 1983, ARPANET split into MILNET, for military use, and ARPANET for academic and scientific research.

What finally plucked the Net from its an academic and military roots and set it on the road to becoming the global phenomenon we now know was the World Wide Web, which was invented in 1989 by Tim Berners-Lee, a British researcher at CERN's European Laboratory for Particle Physics in Switzerland. Berners-Lee also established a standard for addressing (URLs), linking language and transferring multi-media documents on the Web (HTML and HTTP).

In *Weaving the Web*, Berners-Lee tells his story about the invention of the World Wide Web and his role in making the Web the basis of today's communications revolution. What comes over clearly is that he is no self-publicist – his account is modest and his use of language understated

What also comes over is his idealism. An astute man, he certainly appreciated the commercial potential of his invention – John Naughton, writing about Berners-Lee in *The Observer* described him as "a man whose intellectual property rights could have made him richer than Bill Gates and Warren Buffet combined." And yet he turned his back on all that, preferring to work for the common good.

His underpinning optimism emerges clearly in the final chapter of the book, where he writes:

"I do not ... pin my hopes on an overpowering order emerging spontaneously from the chaos. I feel that deliberately to build a society, incrementally, using the best ideas we have, is our duty and will also be the most fun. We are slowly learning the value of decentralized, diverse systems, and of mutual respect and tolerance. Whether you put it down to evolution or your favorite spirit, the neat thing is that we seem as humans to be tuned so that we do in the end get the most fun out of doing the 'right' thing ... If we end up producing a structure in hyperspace that allows us to work together harmoniously, that would be a metamorphosis. Though it would, I hope, happen incrementally, it would result in a huge restructuring of society. A society that could advance with intercreativity and group intuition rather than conflict as the basic mechanism would be a major change.

"If we lay the groundwork right and try novel ways of interacting on the new Web, we may find a whole new set of financial, ethical, cultural and governing structures to which we can choose to belong, rather than having to pick the ones we happen to physically live in. Bit by bit those structures that work best would become more important in the world, and democratic systems might take on different shapes."

But this optimism is tempered by realism. He fully recognizes that the Internet has potential downsides if mishandled. Evan Schwartz, in his book *Digital Darwinism*, records a conversation in which Berners-Lee outlines one of his concerns:

> " 'What if telecom companies start handing out PCs for free to sign you up for Internet service and show you ads?' Actually, this is something that has already happened and it greatly disturbs Berners-Lee. He sees a danger in bundling everything together this way. 'I was brought up on *The Times* of London,' he says, 'which people buy for its editorial independence.' But nowadays, 'the search button on the browser no longer provides an objective search but a commercial one. Hardware comes with software that sells rather than informs.' "

As well as his misgivings about the possible impact of commercial factors on the development of the Net, there are other aspects of Berners-Lee's vision for the Internet that have yet to be fully realized. He hopes, for example, that the Internet will become as much a publications medium as a public information source. He believes that the Net provides an opportunity for individuals to participate actively in building collective knowledge. The surfer would become less a mere viewer of information and more an active, engaged contributor to change, and the Internet would become a medium that can codify the sum total of human knowledge and understanding.

The Web is most powerful not as a mass medium, he suggests, but rather a means for organizing communities, niche markets, and teams within companies. "I'm less happy with the incentive for reaching a global audience," says Berners-Lee. "The good news is that intranets are bringing the technology back into corporations to be used as a group tool."

In the future, he says, the Web will be more fun, will blend better into everyday life, and will be something that doesn't even require computers as we've come to know them. "Your kids will be rummaging through boxes of breakfast cereal," he muses, "and they'll say: 'What is this?' And they'll pull it out and unroll it, and it will be magnetic, and they'll put it on the refrigerator, and start browsing the Web with it."

## The author

Tim Berners-Lee is currently the director of the World Wide Web Consortium (W3C) and is a principal research scientist at the MIT Laboratory for Computer Science. He is widely credited with inventing the World Wide Web in late 1990 while working at CERN, the European Particle Physics Laboratory in Geneva. Prior to working at CERN, he was a founding director of Image Computer Systems, a consultant in hardware and software design, real-time communication graphics and text processing, and a principal engineer with Plessey Telecommunications. He is a graduate of Oxford University.

### Reality check

The primary concern about the Internet as a potential medium for transacting significant levels of commercial business revolves around its security standards. Given the demonstrable ability of computer hackers to penetrate relatively sophisticated and security conscious installations – defense computers and the like – there must be a significant risk that the Internet, which has not to date been overly concerned about issues of confidentiality and information security, could become an easy target for computer fraud.

## Sources and further reading

Berners-Lee, Tim (1999) *Weaving the Web: the Past, Present and Future of the World Wide Web by its Inventor*, Orion Business Books, UK.

Anybody wanting to find out more about the history of the Internet should check out the following sites:
http://info.isoc.org/guest/zakon/Internet/History/HIT.html
http://www.davesite.com/webstation/net-history.shtml
http://www.pbs.org/internet/timeline/

# ALEX BIRCH, PHILIPP GERBERT & DIRK SCHNEIDER

## *The Age of E-tail*

## 2000

D espite recent, well-publicized dot.com failures, you and I know that it would be plain wrong-headed to consign the concept of online commerce to the business recycle bin. Equally, to declare that we are living in the age of e-tail has a distinct whiff of the hyperbolic about it. Nonetheless, the future of some kind of an electronic market place seems assured. Birch, Gerbert and Schneider clearly believe so, and in *The Age of E-tail* they explore 12 key themes that underpin their thinking::

1 *The future of shopping is online.* E-shopping, say the authors, has reached a mass-market audience in the USA and is set to conquer the world from there. For the established retailers and entrepreneurs the critical question is not which sector is ripe for Internet trading, but rather whether the game has already been decided. For example, they say, it is already probably too late to target the books sector in the US unless Amazon.com makes a huge error of judgement.

2 *Traditional physical assets are dead weight.* Established companies must question the fundamentals of their business – otherwise an Internet start-up will do it for them. E-shopping is not about exploiting an additional sales channel, but about establishing a whole new business. Middlemen disappear, as do industry and sector boundaries. Holding an established position becomes an obstacle on a path to the future. Traditional physical retail formats must restructure fundamentally or disappear.

3 *New players are seizing power.* New players are building up a lead in e-shopping. New competitors are springing up everywhere, and competition is becoming increasingly intense. Portals and "market makers" could hold the land rights for the next bonanza.

4 *Survival of the fastest.* The Internet has stimulated a new form of corporate Darwinism in which survival and winning become equivalent. Market leadership and the creation of successful new retail formats are critical. This can be particularly challenging given that most e-shopping sites are loss making on a large scale, due to a combination of high start-up and investment costs and ease with which business models can be emulated by competitors.

5 *Internet shops need new brands.* Traditional brands are diminished on the Internet. UK pension-provider Prudential realized this when they decided to launch an on-line bank. The on-line community represented a new and very different set of target customers to Prudential's traditional base, and needed wooing differently. Egg, the brand they went for, made little of the Pru's traditional virtues – solid, dependable, long-established. Rather the emphasis was on Egg as a brand that was modern, technology-friendly, convenient, and different.

6 *Context makes the difference.* Internet success won't come for operations that are simply cloned from the physical world, particularly if they are no more than extended electronic catalogues. Product availability is no longer an issue – the key to success is to design a retail site around convenience, content that doesn't just describe the product but which adds value (Amazon's use of reader reviews being an example), and building a sense of community and belonging for the customer. Behind these elements though, and critical to a retail site's success, is a far more familiar attribute – commercial nous.

7 *Customer loyalty is important but increasingly difficult to create.* The e-customer is a restless, fickle, volatile entity and yet most e-tailers need repeat business to achieve profitability. Winning loyalty means knowing more about customers and offering more; it means addressing customers individually; it means giving customers control of the business relationship by enabling then to design personalized products (e.g. buying a computer from Dell) or manage transactions themselves (e.g. customers of an on-line bank checking their accounts, making transfers etc.); and it means creating a sense of community, but community from the perspective of customers (they are not interested in maximizing your profits, but have their own interests and needs at heart).

8 *Built-to-order offerings will upset traditional value chains.* There are hardly any limits to personalization. Most cars and PCs are now made to individual specifications – soon all successful e-tailers will offer almost everything tailored individually to the customer. Even

if the product is uniform – one copy of *Harry Potter and the Goblet of Fire* is the same as any other – the surrounding experience can be tailored.

9 *The Internet will pervade every communications device we use.* The Internet is the backbone of the e-tail economy. Connection to the Net is no longer purely via the PC or laptop, connectivity say the authors is tomorrow's watchword. Televisions, mobiles, and other intelligent equipment capable of connection will accelerate the pace of change. The new Web generation – our "net kids" – will be online as a matter of course, and they will have 24-hour access to a host of information and artificial intelligence resources.

10 *Digitizable products will be free.* When products themselves become digital, the marginal cost of production and distribution is zero. With technology like MP3, CD-writers, recordable DVD either with us or just around the corner, we are already seeing the first skirmishes in a guerilla war waged by consumers unwilling to pay for them. Software, music, books and films are first in the firing line. Current legal frameworks will become increasingly inoperable and will collapse.

11 *Innovation will be driven from the duality of product and service.* Duality, in authors' words, is the idea that "each product is a service and each service is a product." As soon as a product becomes capable of being personalized, e.g. a PC, then there is a strong element of service in the transaction – customer needs are analyzed, a machine is built to order, telephones hotlines are available and so on. Conversely, stockbrokers traditionally provided advice to clients, monitored stock performance, reviewed customer portfolios; electronic broking services have essentially "productized" what was previously a service.

12 *Survival requires financing.* Traditional financial markets have a hard time with intangible company values. Equity is the new cash for Internet companies.

As well as exploring these themes in depth, *The Age of E-tail* contains some nice touches. Each chapter contains a "searchlight" summary of key points as well as a list of Websites for the companies highlighted by the authors as examples of good and bad practice. Throughout the book, there are useful tips and wrinkles for the e-tail novice. More crucially, the authors set out a coherent and credible approach to e-tail which speaks as much to the long established bricks and mortar business as it does to the fresh-faced start-up proposition. As a guide to how to enter successfully the world of electronic shopping, it hasn't yet been bettered.

## The authors

Alex Birch is a partner with OC&C in London. His focus area is e-business strategy, working with a range of established and start-up companies on their Internet initiatives in a wide range of business to business and business to consumer sectors.

Philipp Gerbert is a partner with OC&C (The McKenna Group) in Palo Alto, the heart of Silicon Valley His focus is the creation of Internet strategies. He advises companies – from start-ups to multinationals – in technology infrastructure, communications, media and e-commerce at large.

Dirk Schneider is a partner with OC&C in Dusseldorf. He advises clients in the retail, consumer goods, tourism and travel sectors, amongst others. His focus is on strategic growth, marketing and sales. He is co-author of *Marken Power* (Brand Power) published in Germany

### Is e-shopping primarily a US phenomenon?

"The US enjoys a tremendous structural advantage for Internet players. It is the largest homogeneous market (there is no 'Common Market' online in Europe!), has by far the largest online consumer base today and the use of the Web has penetrated everyday life in a much deeper way. In addition, Internet sales in the US receive a subsidy from the absence of sales tax.

"We believe that pure e-shopping players have to succeed in the US first, or they will simply be swallowed by their US counterparts later. But consumers in the rest of the world are embracing the Web quickly. Interestingly some of the US advantages in online plays may be disadvantages when it comes to a combined online/off-line play. The point being that the sales tax regime actually forces companies into a pure online play, preventing most of the 'bricks-and-mortar' players in the US developing consumer-friendly, 'click-and-mortar' (i.e. combined online/off-line) concepts. In the rest of the world the current absence of dominant online players gives traditional companies a better chance of successfully entering the Internet space.

"Sadly, some of these perspectives have triggered the wrong conclusions in traditional companies all over the world. Many view the

Internet merely as a sales channel and treat it as an add-on without fundamentally questioning their current business system.

"They are wrong! The 'Net Imperative' demands that the Internet be embraced as the central medium of the future and companies concentrate on developing truly complementary off-line value (context and convenience, entertainment, customer acquisition and loyalty). Current asset bases should be aggressively transformed, built or divested accordingly. Strangely, in the US pure Web players might actually be the first to develop a winning 'click-and-mortar' proposition offline advertising is the first area to become dominated by them. The rest of the world has been infected by e-shopping, but hopefully in some respects it will leapfrog the development in the US."

Taken from *The Age of E-tail*

## *Sources and further reading*

Birch, Alex, Gerbert, Philipp & Schneider, Dirk (2000) *The Age of E-tail: Conquering the New World of Electronic Shopping*, Capstone, UK. The book has a companion Website, which can be found at www.theageofe-tail.com

# FRANCES CAIRNCROSS

# *The Death of Distance*

## 1997

R| eaders of the *Economist* will be familiar with the work of Frances
Cairncross who has been a senior editor there since 1984.
Those who have read her indispensable surveys on the telecommunications industry will know what to expect. Written in the
same approachable style that makes a high level of technical knowledge
unnecessary, *The Death of Distance* does nothing less than map out how
converging communications technology will reshape the economic,
commercial and political landscape over the next few years.

This is not another narrowly defined book that simply describes
advances in information technology and the communications revolution.
Its territory lies in the practical ramifications of these advances for the
way in which we work and live. It is a journey into a new world, which
tackles the changing nature of organizations, communities, government
authority and culture and languages along the way. It is a staggering
achievement in synthesis helped, no doubt, by access to the formidable
resources of the *Economist*.

Near the start of the book, Cairncross sets outs what she calls "The
Trendspotter's Guide to New Communications" in which she outlines
30 developments in information and communication technology that
will impact on industry and society in the not so distant future, before
going on to discuss each in depth. Here are some of her developments
to watch:

* *The death of distance*. Distance will no longer determine the cost
  of communicating electronically. Companies will organize certain
  types of work in three shifts according to the world's three main
  time zones.

- *The fate of location.* Companies will locate any screen-based activity wherever they can find the best bargain of skills and productivity.
- *The irrelevance of size.* Small companies will offer services that, in the past, only giants could provide. Individuals with valuable ideas will attract global venture capital.
- *More customized content.* Improved networks will also allow individuals to order "content for one."
- *A deluge of information.* Because people's capacity to absorb new information will not increase, they will need filters to sift, process, and edit it.
- *Increased value of brand.* What's hot – whether a product, a personality, a sporting event, or the latest financial data – will attract greater rewards because the potential market will increase greatly. That will create a category of global super-rich, many of them musicians, actors, artists, athletes, and investors.
- *Communities of practice.* Common interests, experiences, and pursuits rather than proximity will bind communities together.
- *The loose-knit corporation.* Many companies will become networks of independent specialists; more employees will therefore work in smaller units or alone.
- *More minnows, more giants.* On one hand, the cost of starting new businesses will decline, and companies will more easily buy in services so that more small companies will spring up. On the other, communication amplifies the strength of brands and the power of networks.
- *The proliferation of ideas.* New ideas and information will travel faster to the remotest corners of the world. Third world countries will have access to knowledge that the industrial world has long enjoyed.
- *The shift from government policing to self-policing.* As content sweeps across national borders, it will be harder to enforce laws banning child pornography, libel, and other criminal or subversive material and those protecting copyright and other intellectual property.
- *Redistribution of wages.* Low-wage competition will reduce the earning power of many people in rich countries employed in routine screen-based tasks, but the premium for certain skills will grow. People with skills that are in demand will earn broadly similar amounts wherever they live in the world. So income differences within countries will grow; and income differences between countries will narrow.
- *Less need for immigration and emigration.* Poor countries with good communications technology will be able to retain their skilled

### Zeitbite

"The death of distance as a determinant of the cost of communications will probably be the single most important economic force shaping society in the first half of the next century. It will alter, in ways that are only dimly imaginable, decisions about where people live and work; concepts of national borders; patterns of international trade."

Frances Cairncross, in a 1995 survey of the telecommunications industry published in the *Economist*

workers, who will be less likely to emigrate to countries with higher costs of living if they can earn rich-world wages and pay poor-world prices for everyday necessities right at home.

- *A market for citizens.* The greater freedom to locate anywhere and earn a living will hinder taxation. Countries will compete to bid down tax rates and to attract businesses, savers, and wealthy residents.
- *Rebalance of political power.* Rulers and representatives will become more sensitive to lobbying and public-opinion polls, especially in established democracies.
- *Global peace.* As countries become even more economically interdependent, people will communicate more freely and learn more about the ideas and aspirations of human beings in other parts of the globe. The effect will be to increase understanding, foster tolerance, and ultimately promote worldwide peace.

In the five years since the book was published, some of the specific, technology-based phenomena that she predicted have come to pass. Some developing countries, for example, now routinely perform on-line services – monitoring security screens, running help-lines and call centers, writing software, and so forth. Much of the social and political change she anticipated, however, has yet to show through to any meaningful level. And global peace seems as far away now as it did in 1995.

Yet in truth, the value of *The Death of Distance* does not rest in whether Cairncross has a good accuracy rate with her predictions. Like any good history of the future, the value lies more in the extent to which Cairncross manages to challenge assumptions and provoke our thinking.

By that measure, most people will still today find this book well worth reading as a primer for what may lie ahead.

## The author

Frances Cairncross is a senior editor at the *Economist*, where she has worked since 1984. She is a Governor of the National Institute of Economic and Social Research, and is a presenter on the BBC's Analysis program. Previous books have included *Costing the Earth* and *Green Inc.*

## Sources and further reading

Cairncross, Frances (1997) *The Death of Distance*, Orion Publishing, UK.
The *Economist* Website can be found at www.economist.com

# MANUEL CASTELLS

# The Information Age: Economy, Society and Culture

Volume I: *The Rise of the Network Society* **1996**

Volume II: *The Power of Identity* **1997**

Volume III: *End of Millennium* **1998**

K evin Kelly, writing in *New Rules for the New Economy*, describes Manuel Castells as "a sociologist with a European's bent for the large-scale sweep of history." In an age when all too many new economy texts stretch a meager handful of barely original insights beyond breaking point, Castells' sprawling, literate, visionary and densely argued trilogy is like trading up from the bargain red in the local supermarket to a classy Bordeaux. It's rich, complex, and improving with age.

In *The Rise of the Network Society*, the first of three linked investigations of contemporary global, economic, political and social change, he offers a catalogue of evidence for the arrival of a new global, networked-based culture. For Castells, the Network Society is characterized by, amongst other things:

- the globalization of strategically decisive economic activities;
- the networking form of organization; and
- the flexibility and instability of work, and the individualization of labor.

The book goes on to examine the processes of globalization that have marginalized whole countries and peoples by leaving them excluded from informational networks.

Some of his specific findings:

- There is no systematic structural relationship between the diffusion of information technologies and the evolution of unemployment levels in the economy as a whole.
- Although the communications revolution enables the global distribution of major events, particularly sporting set pieces like the Olympics or World Cup, in general we live, not in a global village but rather in customized cottages globally produced and locally distributed.
- The multimedia world is increasingly populated by two distinct populations – the interacting and the interacted i.e. those who are able to select their communication options and those who are provided with a restricted number of prepackaged choices.
- The new global economy and the emerging informational society are spawning a new urban form – megacities, cities with populations of anything from ten million to 20 million. Size, though, is not their defining quality; rather their significance rests in their capacity to function as nodes of the global economy, concentrating media and political power, acting as magnets for regional resources, and linking up the informational networks.

In Volume II, *The Power of Identity*, Castells gives his account of two conflicting trends shaping the world: globalization and identity. The book describes proactive movements, such as feminism and environmentalism, and reactive movements that build trenches of resistance on behalf of God, nation, ethnicity, family or locality. The final volume of a trilogy, *End of Millennium*, is devoted to processes of global social change induced by interaction between networks and identity.

Having studiously refused for virtually all of the three volumes to engage in futurology, Castells concludes the final volume of the trilogy by setting out "some trends that may configure society in the early twenty-first century." His key predictions that we may well see are:

- the information technology revolution accelerating its transformative potential, and as a result technology will achieve its potential to unleash productivity;
- the full flowering of the genetic revolution;
- the continuing and relentless expansion of the global economy;
- the survival of nation states, but not necessarily their sovereignty; and
- the "exclusion of the excluders by the excluded," i.e. those that do not have the capability to participate in the information economy will become more tribal in outlook.

**Zeitbite**

"The twenty-first century will not be a dark age. Neither will it deliver to most people the bounties promised by the most extraordinary technological revolution in history. Rather, it may well be characterized by informed bewilderment."

Manuel Castells, *The Information Age*

Although Castells voices a number of concerns throughout the three volumes of *The Information Age*, he concludes his trilogy on a cautiously optimistic note.

"The promise of the Information Age is the unleashing of unprecedented productive capacity by the power of the mind. I think, therefore I produce. In so doing, we will have the leisure to experiment with spirituality, and the opportunity of reconciliation with nature, without sacrificing the material well-being of our children. The dream of the Enlightenment, that reason and science would solve the problems of humankind, is within reach. Yet there is an extraordinary gap between our technological overdevelopment and our social underdevelopment. Our economy, society, and culture are built on interests, values, institutions, and systems of representation that, by and large, limit collective creativity, confiscate the harvest of information technology, and deviate our energy into self-destructive confrontation. This state of affairs must not be. There is no eternal evil in human nature. There is nothing that cannot be changed by conscious, purposive social action, provided with information, and supported by legitimacy. If people are informed, active, and communicate throughout the world; if business assumes its social responsibility; if the media become the messengers, rather than the message; if political actors react against cynicism, and restore belief in democracy; if culture is reconstructed from experience; if humankind feels the solidarity of the species throughout the globe; if we assert intergenerational solidarity by living in harmony nature; if we depart for the exploration of our inner self, having made peace among ourselves. If all this is made possible by our informed, conscious, shared decision, while there is still time, maybe then, we may, at last, be able to live and let live, love and be loved."

How then to sum up this trilogy? First of all, it has to be said that this is not a book to skim-read on the train (believe me, I tried) – Castells is a large canvas thinker, the three books run to almost 1500 pages, and the text and style often fit what you might expect from a European academic! That said, and even if he goes occasionally into over-exhaustive detail, Castells writes with intelligence and obvious insight. For a systematic interpretation of the global information economy world at the turn of the millennium, Castells has no equal.

## The author

Recognized as one of the world's leading social thinkers and research-ers, Manuel Castells is Professor of Sociology, and of Planning at the University of California, Berkeley, where he was appointed in 1979. Prior to this, he spent 12 years teaching at the University of Paris. He has published over 20 books. Castells was born in Spain in 1942.

## Sources and further reading

Castells, Manuel, *The Information Age: Economy, Society and Culture*,
Blackwell Publishers Ltd, UK.
Volume I: *The Rise of the Network Society* (1996)
Volume II: *The Power of Identity* (1997)
Volume III: *End of Millennium* (1998)

Castells has contributed a 22-page essay entitled "Information Technol-ogy and Global Capitalism" to a collection edited by Will Hutton and Anthony Giddens called *On the Edge: Living with Global Capitalism* (Cape, 2000).

# JAMES COLLINS & JERRY PORRAS

## *Built to Last*

## 1994

hen *Built to Last* appeared in 1994, it was the product of a six-year investigation by James Collins and Jerry Porras, both Stanford professors at the time, which set out to uncover the underlying principles that could yield enduring, great companies. For the book, they examined 18 companies that had significantly outperformed the general stock market over a number of decades. The companies looked at included Disney, General Electric, Hewlett-Packard, IBM, and Wal-Mart

The key finding to emerge from their research was that, in their words, "the fundamental distinguishing characteristic of the most enduring and successful corporations is that they preserve a cherished core ideology while simultaneously stimulating progress and change in everything that is not part of their core ideology. Put another way, they distinguish their timeless core values and enduring core purpose (which should never change) from their operating practices and business strategies (which should be changing constantly in response to a changing world). In truly great companies, change is a constant, but not the only constant. They understand the difference between what should never change and what should be open for change, between what is truly sacred and what is not. And by being clear about what should never change, they are better able to stimulate change and progress in everything else."

For Collins and Porras, the essence of greatness does not lie in cost cutting, restructuring, or the pure profit motive. It lies in people's dedication to building companies around a sense of purpose and around core values that infuse work with the kind of meaning that goes beyond just making a profit. Truly great companies, they claim, immerse their people in the core ideology. At Disney, for example, where their workers are "cast members" rather than employees, the language and day to day rituals of the organization act as an ongoing reinforcement of the values of the company.

But the clinching argument for them is in the evidence they found that those companies with a strong core ideology and which opted to make a lasting contribution also make more money than their more pragmatic, short-termist rivals in the end.

So what's this got to do with the new economy? Well, implicit on every page of *Built to Last* is a simple question – why would a company settle for creating something mediocre that does little more than make money, when it could create something outstanding that makes a lasting contribution as well? At a time when it seems the lifespan of some dot.com companies can be measured in weeks or months rather than decades, this question strikes at the heart of business and life in the New Economy.

Even as Collins and Porras were preparing their findings in the early nineties, in fact entrepreneurs have followed a Silicon Valley paradigm since the seventies – a set of assumptions about how to handle a startup. The model is very simple: come up with a good idea, raise venture capital, grow as quickly as you can, and then go public or sell up. Above all, though, do it at speed. Even 20 years ago, a company that hadn't made it big within 7 to 10 years was deemed a failure. There was also at that time an ethic of impermanence: the Silicon Valley business culture generally had no expectation that a company would be built to last.

By today's standards of short-termism Silicon Valley-style, that time frame seems positively snail-like. By today's standards, entrepreneurs like Bill Hewlett and Dave Packard, co-founders of Hewlett-Packard, or Sam Walton, founder of Wal-Mart, look like relics of a bygone business era.

Aware that much of what is currently going on in the new economy seems to undermine the validity of the findings of *Built to Last*, James Collins faced the criticism head-on in an article he wrote for *Fast Company* magazine provocatively titled "Built to Flip." In the article, he tells a story that gives an insight into the 21st century entrepreneurial mindset:

"Not long ago, I gave a seminar to a group of 20 entrepreneurial CEOs who had gathered at my Boulder, Colorado management lab to learn about my most recent research. I tried to begin with a quick review of *Built to Last* findings, but almost immediately a chorus of objections rang out from the group:

'What does 'building to last' have to do with what we face today?"

"Built to flip" is an intriguing idea. As Collins describes it:

"No need to build a company, much less one with enduring value. Today, it's enough to pull together a good story, to implement the rough draft of an idea, and – presto! – instant wealth … In the built-to-flip world, the notion of investing persistent effort in order to build a great company seems, well, quaint, unnecessary – even stupid."

He goes on:

"Have we labored to build something better than what members of previous generations built – only to find their faces staring back at us in the mirror? Is the biggest flip of all the flip that transforms the once-promising spirit of the new economy back into the tired skin of the old economy?"

Encouragingly, he concludes that "Built to flip" is itself not built to last. He puts his faith in a combination of the underlying logic of the market place and the nature of the human spirit:

"Built to Flip can't last. Ultimately, it cannot become the dominant model. Markets are remarkably efficient: In the long run, they reward actual contribution, even though short-run market bubbles can divert excess capital to non-contributors. Over time, the marketplace will crush any model that does not produce real results. Its self-correcting mechanisms will ensure the brutal fairness on which our social stability rests.

   "The most significant consequence of the Built to Flip model isn't socioeconomic, however. It is personal. When it emerged in the early 1980s, the new-economy culture rested on three primary tenets: freedom and self-direction in your work; purpose and contribution through your work; and wealth creation by your work. Central to that culture was the belief that work is our primary activity and that through work we can achieve the sense of meaning that we are looking for in life. Driving the new economy were immensely talented, highly energetic people who sought a practical answer to a fundamen-

**Zeitbite**

The creative drive behind the new economy at its best has been superseded by a way of thinking that recalls the 1980s at its worst: a Wall Street-like culture that celebrates the twin propositions that "greed is good" and that "more is better." The hard truth is that we're dangerously close to killing the soul of the new economy. Even worse, we're in danger of becoming the very thing that we defined ourselves in opposition to. Those who kindled the spirit of the new economy rejected the notion of working just for money; today, we seem to think that it's fine to work just for money – as long as it's a lot of money.

Taken from "Built to flip" by James Collins

tal question: How can I create work that I'm passionate about, that makes a contribution, and that makes money?

By fostering a culture of entitlement, Built to Flip debases the very concept of meaningful work. And, as is always the case with any form of entitlement, it ultimately debases the person who feels entitled."

Let's hope that Collins is right. Let's hope that founders of new economy businesses come to realize that it is better to concentrate primarily on building an organization rather than on hitting a market just right with a visionary product idea and riding the growth curve of an attractive product cycle. Let's hope that the primary output of their efforts is the tangible implementation of a great and sustainable idea and that their greatest creation is the company itself and what it stands for.

And finally, let's hope that 21st century entrepreneurs find value in Collins and Porras' analysis of which corporate cultures worked at the end of the 20th century, and that they recognize *Built to Last* as a book they simply cannot ignore.

### Reality check: built to be short-lived

"There are at least two categories of companies that should not be built to last.

"The first category is 'the company as disposable injection device.' In this model, the company is simply a throwaway vessel, a means of developing and injecting a new product or an innovative technology into the world. Most biotechnology and medical-device ventures fall into this category. They function as a highly decentralized form of large company R&D – in effect, serving as external labs for one or another of the large, powerful pharmaceutical companies that dominate the world market. With most such ventures, the only question is which large company will end up owning a given technology.

"One example: Cardiometrics Inc., a Mountain View, California company that set itself up in 1985 for the purpose of developing a device that could gather data on the actual extent of coronary disease in a patient. (The goal was to reduce the number of people who undergo unnecessary bypass surgery.) Cardiometrics was not built to last, and in 1997 it was acquired by EndoSonics Corp., a heart-catheter company in Rancho Cordova, California that has a distribution network capable of reaching millions of patients. In this case, acquisition by another company made perfect sense – economically, organizationally, strategically, entrepreneurially. And the acquisition in no way demeaned the contribution that the founders and employees of Cardiometrics had made in developing a vital new technology. For companies like this one, it is eminently reasonable to do the hard work of creating a product that can make a distinctive contribution – and then to sell the product to a company that can leverage it faster, cheaper, and better. In retrospect, we can all point to companies that should have viewed themselves as 'built not to last.' Confronting that reality would have helped them understand that they were never more than a project, a product, or a technology. Lotus, VisiCorp, Netscape, Syntex, Coleco – all of these companies would have served themselves and the world better if they had accepted their limited purpose from the outset. Ultimately, they squandered time and resources that might have been applied more efficiently elsewhere.

"The second category is 'the company as platform for a genius.' In this model, the company is a tool for magnifying and extending the creative drive of one remarkable individual – a visionary who has immense talent but lacks the temperament required to build an enduring, great company. Once that person is gone, so is the company's reason for being. The best historical example is Thomas Edison's R&D laboratory. The purpose of that enterprise was to leverage Edison's creative genius: Edison would spin his ideas and then flip them out to people who could build companies around them. That's what he did with the lightbulb, and that's how General Electric came into being. When Edison died, his R&D laboratory died with him – as indeed it should have.

Taken from James Collins, "Built to flip," published in *Fast Company*

## The authors

James Collins runs a management learning laboratory in Boulder, Colorado and is a visiting professor at the University of Virginia. He has also taught at Stanford and worked at McKinsey and Hewlett-Packard. He can be contacted at JCC512@aol.com

Jerry I. Porras is the Fred H. Merrill Professor of Organizational Behavior and Change at Stanford University Graduate School of Business. He has been based at Stanford since 1972. Prior to that he was in the US Army and worked at Lockheed and General Electric. His contact details are Porras_Jerry@GSB.Stanford.edu

## Sources and further reading

Collins, James C. and Porras, Jerry I. (1994) *Built to last*, Harper Business, New York.
Collins, James C. (March 2000) Built to flip, *Fast Company*, Issue 32.

# DIANE COYLE

## The Weightless World

## 1997

few years ago, Nicholas Negroponte of MIT described how the emphasis in world trade was increasingly shifting from the physical transport of atoms to the electronic transfer of bits.

In *The Weightless World*, Diane Coyle, who is economics editor at the *Independent*, maps out today's economic and social landscape in a world increasingly transformed by the digital revolution, not to mention globalism and the disappearance of many of the old securities.

For Coyle, weightlessness is a "symbol of the economic effects of the clusters of advances in information and communication technology," and the financial markets "the ultimate embodiment of weightlessness, or in other words the intangibility of an increasing proportion of modern economies."

What gives the concept particular potency is the manner in which technological change interacts with other fundamental changes like demographic and social trends and the grand sweep of social history, creating, in Coyle's word's, "the age of insecurity."

This is not a "how-to" book for business people, nor is Coyle particularly concerned about the new technology itself. She has far bigger fish to fry. What distinguishes *The Weightless World* from most new economy books is its focus on the economic and political consequences of new technology. The book discusses the impact of weightlessness on, *inter alia*, welfare, economic policy, and particularly on the process and scope of government – both nationally and internationally. For her, the interesting question is how, at the level of detailed policy interventions, governments can equip their voters to prosper in a world of rapid and unpredictable economic change.

This, she writes, "involves a debate about international co-operation on trade and investment in the face of continuing globalization. It also means policy-makers must recognize the links between their regulatory and ethical frameworks and the level of economic prosperity they can deliver. And regulation, too, has to be increasingly international. To take another highly topical example, as the US permits the growing of genetically modified foodstuffs, it will be hard for European governments to prevent their import without the active sympathy and co-operation of the American government. A modified tomato can only be identified if its grower agrees to label it, which requires the American government to enforce the labelling desired by the Europeans."

She continues: "For the use of knowledge is not easily restricted and bounded. The weightless world will force a radical rethink about how prosperity increases and what governments can do to help rather than hinder it."

There are signs that governments are beginning to learn, if still reluctantly, the lesson that many big companies have taken on board; that it is no longer appropriate, perhaps even possible, to run the show from the center. Decentralization and dispersion are the keys to survival.

Coyle's achievement in *The Weightless World* is that she brings a perceptive and critical eye to the downsides of the new economy. This is not a depressing commentary though – she doesn't believe that we are necessarily heading for a 21st-century economic apocalypse.

Her conclusions are sobering rather than pessimistic. As she writes towards the end of the book, "What we ... face ..., as in the last industrial revolution, is a mammoth problem of transition and distribution. The world is a riskier place. People in the industrialised world are ill-equipped to deal with their loss of security and are governed by profoundly undemocratic economic institutions. Individuals must have a greater stake in shaping their own future if they are to be equipped to cope with new economic uncertainties."

This requires no less than "a redrafting of the economic policy map." She adds: "Just as the political importance of the nation state has declined, so has its economic influence. Policies need to be shaped internationally and locally as well as nationally. This is a debate whose resonances are obvious in Europe, where the structure of power in the EU and its defenses against the outside world are amongst the most bitterly contested political issues. But it is just as important in North America, where anti-government, anti-federal and anti-international forces are gaining strength."

Anybody who values peace and economic progress has to hope that the wake-up call contained in *The Weightless World* is heeded. The evidence for that happening is decidedly mixed. Nonetheless, Coyle has brought together the arguments brilliantly in this cogent and provocative commentary.

## The author

Diane Coyle is Economics Editor of the *Independent*

## Sources and further reading

Coyle, Diane (1997) *The Weightless World*, Capstone, UK.

# STAN DAVIS & CHRISTOPHER MEYER

## *Blur*

## 1998

I n recent years, as the world has grown ever more complicated and confusing, business books have started to lose their sense of certainty. From *The Principles of Scientific Management* by Frederick Taylor, published in 1911, to *Competitive Strategy* by Michael Porter, which first appeared in 1980, business books carried an air of authority. But just as "Trust me, I'm a doctor" has lost its convincing resonance in the light of numerous medical scandals, so Taylor's idea of "the one best way" to tackle management and corporate issues no longer convinces. Management thinkers these days offer paradox instead of placebos or paracetamol.

So it is with *Blur*, a book in which Davis and Meyer are absolutely up-front about the state of their thinking: "We are not offering the ultimate word on our topics, but a starting point: provocative ideas, observations, and predictions to get you to think creatively about your business and your future."

The authors, who are both based at the Ernst & Young Center for Business Innovation in Boston, maintain that "connectivity, speed, and the growth of intangible value" have catapulted business into a period of unprecedented transition that demands immediate and creative attention.

These three elements in combination, say Davis and Meyer, "are blurring the rules and redefining our businesses and our lives. They are destroying solutions, such as mass production, segmented pricing, and standardized jobs, that worked for the relatively slow, unconnected industrial world."

## The BLUR Equation

Speed × Connectivity × Intangibles = BLUR
**Speed:** every aspect of business and the connected organization operates and changes in real time.
**Connectivity:** everything is becoming electronically connected to everything else: products, people, companies, countries, everything.
**Intangibles:** every offer has both tangible and intangible economic value. The intangible is growing faster.
**BLUR:** the new world in which you will come to live and work.

Taken from *Blur*

Ignore these forces at your peril, they warn: harness and leverage them, "and you can enter the world of BLUR, move to its cadence and once again see the world clearly." To achieve this clarity, it is necessary to see where the forces of blur are having an impact. The authors explore three particular areas: the blur of desires; the blur of fulfillment; and the blur of resources.

1   *The BLUR of desires.* The demand side of an economy, "where products and services meld into one to become an offer, and where the roles of buyers and sellers merge into an exchange." Amazon exemplifies both: buy a book and we'll get it delivered to your door, and you tell us what you think about one book and see what others have made of books you have yet to read.

2   *The BLUR of fulfillment.* "Where strategies and organizations dissolve into economic webs and permeable relationships." This creates a new economic model in which "returns increase rather than diminish; supermarkets mimic stock markets; and you want the market – not your strategy – to price, market and manage your offer."

3   *The BLUR of resources.* "Where people are no longer divided into their working and consuming selves, and where capital is more often a liability than an asset. These resources are shaking off their traditional meanings as vigorously as a dog shakes off water after climbing out of a lake." This is demonstrated in the emergence of the idea of intellectual capital as a resource that can be more crucial to a company's survival than more traditional assets. There is also a sense here of the merging of work life and life life.

Davis and Meyer give numerous examples of the way in which traditional boundaries between product and service, capital and people, and buyer and seller are now blurred.

Davis and Meyer contend that blurring offers fresh challenges that should help companies thrive in a changing environment. To help companies and individuals come to terms with operating in a blurred world, they conclude their book by distilling their ideas into "50 ways to BLUR your business." Some examples: Make speed your mindset; Connect everything with everything; Grow your intangibles faster than your tangibles; Manage all business in real time; Be able to do anything you do at anytime, anyplace; Put your offer online and make it interactive; Customize every offer; Don't grow what you can buy; Assume everything will be deregulated; Be big and small simultaneously; Use it, don't own it. If you do own it, use it up; Prize intellectual assets most, financial assets second, physical assets least; and Pay attention – attention is the next scarce resource

They also have some advice for individuals, recommending that we should consider. Their ten ways to blur yourself include giving away knowledge to get more back; create something new constantly; sell your value on the Web; let the market, not the company, determine your worth; become a free agent while still on a payroll; and brand yourself – there's equity there.

There are, then, very positive steps that we can take, organizationally and individually, to successfully negotiate the blurred world. That standing still and doing nothing seems to be the most dangerous response of all is a paradox that Davis and Meyer would probably relish.

## The authors

Stan Davis is a Massachusetts-based writer and speaker. He is Senior Research Fellow at the Ernst & Young Center for Business Innovation in Cambridge, Massachusetts.

Christopher Meyer is the Director of the Center for Business Innovation, a Partner in Ernst Young, and President of Bios GP, a venture that applies complexity theory to business.

## Sources and further reading

Davis, Stan and Meyer, Chris (1998) *Blur: The Speed of Change in the Connected Economy*, Addison-Wesley, USA.

Davis, Stan and Meyer, Chris (2000) *Future Wealth*, Harvard Business School Press, USA.

In *Future Wealth* – described as the companion volume to *Blur* – Davis and Meyer identify three major consequences of the newly connected economy:

1   risk as opportunity, not only as threat;
2   the growing efficiency of financial markets for human capital; and
3   the need for new forms of social capital.

They go on to explain why they think we are headed toward a new stage of economic development in which "human and intellectual capital [is] the most highly valued resource."

Davis, Stan (1996) *Future Perfect* (10th anniversary edition), Addison Wesley, USA.

# MICHAEL DELL

## *Direct from Dell*

### 1999

I f a storyline of "precocious child becomes successful business leader" has you reaching for the corporate sickbag, then you'll need to approach *Direct from Dell* with care. At the age of 12, Michael Dell earned $2000 selling stamps, and by the time he was 18, he was selling customized personal computers. He started the Dell Computer Corporation in 1985 with $1000, dropping out of his biology course at Austin University in Texas. The company, under his leadership, has gone on to become one of the most successful computer businesses in the world, redefining the industry with its direct-sale approach and the customer support model it pioneered.

Rebecca Saunders, in her insightful book *Business the Dell Way*, attributes Dell's success to ten key factors:

1  *Sell direct.* Dell eliminates the middleman by custom-building IBM clones and selling them directly to consumers, thereby reducing overhead costs and eliminating dealer mark-ups. This is the original marketing concept behind Dell Computer.
2  *Value and manage inventory.* This is a direct consequence of Dell's sell and build approach to manufacture of PCs.
3  *Don't grow for growth's sake.* Dell learned this the hard way. In the early nineties, Dell Computer experienced several expansion problems, including failure of a line of low-quality laptops. Growth is good, but it's controlled growth.
4  *Innovate or evaporate.* Equally, recognize that gradual improvements to each product line reduces risk and allows you to take advantage of rapid technological developments.
5  *Market innovation.* Dell was the first firm to market PCs by phone but now actively encourages business via the Web. Be alert to opportunities outside of traditional distribution channels.

6 *Think and act global.* A young Dell Computer – and young Michael Dell – established the first of 12 international operations. He took his firm abroad almost a decade before most technology companies.

7 *Don't focus on computers, focus on customers and their needs.* Dell believes in going to where customers do business to understand their needs.

8 *Ally with employees.* Hire those who can generate ideas, train people to be creative, and create an environment that allows ideas to be tested.

9 *Ally with suppliers.* Highest quality comes from outsourcing the manufacture of parts to suppliers with most expertise, experience, and quality in producing that part.

10 *Stay the course.* If the formula works, don't mess with it. Dell has been called a "methodical optimizer," someone who comes up with a good idea, recognizes it as such, then tirelessly pursues that idea, examples being the Dell approach to sell and build and lean manufacture.

In *Direct from Dell*, Michael Dell shares his business strategies and offers his thoughts about doing business in the information age. As to the future, Dell believes that the PC marketplace still has some way to go before alternative routes into the Internet – via television, etc. – undermine the need for desktop technology.

The book represents a useful reiteration of Dell's business philosophy and the main elements – eliminate middlemen, build machines to order rather than hold a stockpile, focus on making cheap but high quality PCs and so on – remain sound principles for any direct sales organization setting up in the new economy.

Michael Dell has undoubtedly played his part in building the global PC market. There is though, in the final analysis, a lingering sense that *Direct from Dell* is fundamentally an exercise in corporate spin and a real question mark lingers over whether Dell will be as significant to the future of the new economy as he has been in helping to bring it about.

### Reality check

"The pay of Michael Dell, the founder and chief executive of Dell Computer, tumbled 85 percent last year, to $16.6 million, as the company, the No. 1 direct seller of personal computers, wrestled with its worst performance in six years."

Source: http://www.nytimes.com/library/tech/00/05/biztech/articles/
31dell.html31/05/00

## The author

Texan billionaire Michael Dell is Chairman and Chief Executive Officer of Dell Computer Corporation, the company he founded in 1984 with $1000 in start-up capital. He is a member of the Board of Directors of the United States Chamber of Commerce and the Computerworld/Smithsonian Awards.

## Sources and further reading

Dell, Michael (1999) *Direct from Dell*, HarperBusiness, USA.
Saunders, Rebecca (1999) *Business the Dell Way*, Capstone, UK.

### How to hone your competitive edge the Dell way

- *Think about the customer, not the competition.* Competitors represent your industry's past, as, over the years, collective habits become ingrained. Customers are your future, representing new opportunities, ideas, and avenues for growth.
- *Work to maintain a healthy sense of urgency and crisis.* This doesn't mean that you want to fabricate deadlines or keep people so stressed that they quickly burn out. Set the bar slightly higher than you normally would, so that your people can achieve aggressive goals by working smarter.
- *Turn your competition's greatest strength into a weakness.* Much as every great athlete has an Achilles' heel, so, too, do all great companies. Study the competition's "game": Exploit its weakness by exposing its greatest strength.
- *Be opportunistic, but also be fast.* Look to find opportunity, especially when it isn't readily apparent. Focusing on the customer doesn't mean that you should ignore the competition. If something that your competition did or didn't do provided you with an opportunity today, would you recognize it and be able to act on it immediately? Today a competitive win can be decided literally one day at a time. You have to act fast, be ready, then be ready to change – fast.
- *Swing for hits, not home runs.* Business is like baseball. Go for the highest batting average rather than trying to hit a home run every time. If your competitor is batting .300, you want to bat .350 or

.400. No one's batting 1.000, so you can't worry about it. What you want to focus on is being the best as often as you can. Because there's no such thing as a grand slam product or technology that lasts forever, your competitive edge must come from strategic execution, and from gaining knowledge, studying the economics of your business, and ensuring the flow of information throughout your organization.

- *Be the hunter, not the hunted.* Success is a dangerous thing, as we are at once invincible and vulnerable. Always strive to keep your team focused on growing the business and on winning and acquiring new business. Even though your company may be leading the market, you never want your people to act as though you are. That leads to complacency, and complacency kills. Encourage people to think, "This is good. This worked. Now how can we take what we've proven and rise it to win new business?" There's a big difference between asking that and asking, "How can we defend our existing accounts?"

Taken from *Direct from Dell*

# LARRY DOWNES & CHUNKA MUI

## *Unleashing the Killer App*

### 1998

Q:  What do longbows, lightbulbs, Model Ts and atomic bombs have in common?

A:  They are all inventions whose impact has extended far beyond the activities for which their creators made them. They are killer apps.

ownes and Mui define a killer app as "a new good or service that establishes an entirely new category and, by being first, dominates it, returning several hundred percent on the initial investment … Killer apps are the Holy Grail of technology investors, the stuff of which their silicon dreams are made."

For most companies, killer apps are viewed with mixed feelings. Like as not, say the authors, "killer apps wind up displacing unrelated older offerings, destroying and re-creating industries far from their immediate use, and throwing into disarray the complex relationships between business partners, competitors, customers, and regulators of markets."

Killer apps have the potential to earn enormous sums of money and to re-energize stale economic sector. But, warn Downes and Mui, "like the Hindu god Shiva, they are both regenerative and destructive. It is not for nothing that they are called killer apps." Companies, they go on, are "likely to be bumped off."

Today's killer apps spring mainly from the digital realm, i.e. from the transformation of information into digital form, where it can be manipulated by computers and transmitted by networks. Over the past ten years, the World Wide Web, personal computers, e-mail and most recently mobile phone technology have reshaped (and will continue to profoundly influence) both our working and social worlds in ways that we are still grappling to come to terms with.

The driving force behind killers apps is the remarkable science of semiconductors, which has shifted the world's economy from an industrial to an information base in a little over a quarter of a century. Against this backdrop, Downes and Mui claim that a combination of two laws is driving the proliferation of killer apps – Moore's Law and Metcalfe's Law:

> "The unrelenting, exponential improvements in semiconductor speed, size, and cost that have operated since the 1960s follow Moore's Law, a prediction by Intel founder Gordon Moore that every eighteen months, for the foreseeable future, chip density (and hence computing power) would double while cost remained constant, creating ever more powerful computing devices without raising their price. Announcements from IBM and Intel in late 1997 suggest that Moore's Law may even underpredict the improvement for the next several years. Similar phenomena have been observed by Gordon Bell in data storage and communications bandwidth. The bottom line is simple but potent: faster, cheaper, smaller.
>
> "Less well known than Moore's Law is the observation made by Robert Metcalfe, founder of 3Com Corporation, that networks (whether of telephones, computers, or people) dramatically increase in value with each additional node or user. Metcalfe's Law values the utility of a network as the square of the number of its users, and can be easily appreciated by considering the impact of standard railroad gauges, Morse code, and standardized electrical outlets in the last century and telephones, fax machines, and the Ethernet and Internet protocols today. Once a standard has achieved critical mass, its value to everyone multiplies exponentially."

Moore's Law and Metcalfe's Law found their apotheosis in the Internet. Moore provided the computing power to create new applications, and Moore the growth hormone to extend the level of participation.

These two laws are fundamentally changing how businesses interact with each other and with their customers. Software companies, for example, habitually make new products and standards available at no cost via the Internet in order to reach critical mass more quickly. The business logic is straightforward: achieving critical mass today pre-disposes future users to adopt products with increased enthusiasm and thereby opens up access to potential marginal revenue. Another example of the two laws in tandem is the growth of computing devices with Internet connections – video games, personal digital assistants, mobile phones etc. – users beget users.

Against this backdrop, organizations, from entrepreneurial start-ups to mega-corporations, are coming to realize that the killer app universe will only accommodate two groups – those that master or nurture killer apps and those that fall victim to them. Not surprisingly, Downes and Mui commend membership of the former group and in the book outline 12 points (see opposite) for designing a digital strategy to help identify and create killer apps in an organization.

Implicit in their concept of digital strategy is a view that the classical approach to strategy – top-down, analytical, based on a thorough understanding of the market place, executing carefully developed plans over a period of time – has little place in a killer app universe. Digital strategy has two guiding principles: the first is that the best way to predict the future is to invent it, and the second suggests that the future is unknowable beyond – at most – a 12–18 month time frame, that strategy therefore needs to become a real-time, dynamic, intuitive process.

Downes and Mui have, in *Unleashing the killer app*, provided budding digital strategists with a useful set of lenses for understanding the new e-conomy, as well as some convincing advice about how to prosper in the digital world.

But be warned – below the surface there is a more disquieting message. No matter what your company does or its size or market position, there's probably a killer app lurking out there somewhere that will redefine your business world.

## The 12 principles of killer app design

### Reshaping the landscape

1 *Outsource to the customer.* For example, build an interface into your information sources and give customers the tools to navigate and customize them. Customers provide you with their data – it's more accurate and cheaply gathered.
2 *Cannibalize your markets.* Online newspapers, for example, may reduce sales of print editions, but this loss is balanced against the unrealized power of other information assets that can be exploited in cyberspace.

3 *Treat each customer as a market segment of one.* Cyberspace lends itself to mass customization.

4 *Create communities of value.* Nurture relationships both with and between customers.

## Building new connections

5 *Replace rude interfaces with learning interfaces.* For example, by giving the customer what they want rather than what they would accept.

6 *Ensure continuity for the customer, not yourself.* Customers don't know or don't care when technology replaces familiar ways of doing things as the interface looks the same e.g. digital gauges on car dashboards.

7 *Give away as much information as you can.* The age of closed information systems is over.

8 *Structure every transaction as a joint venture.* For example, larger organizations need to learn how to buy, sell, partner and compete with a new breed of virtual firms.

## Redefining the interior

9 *Treat your assets as liabilities.* Reduce physical assets, build up intangible assets.

10 *Destroy your value chain ...* before your competitors do. Pay particular attention to the declining need for intermediaries.

11 *Manage innovation as a portfolio of options.* Retain flexibility about the best ideas and the best way to implement them.

12 *Hire the children.* They are the natives of cyberspace – incorporate their values, energy and mindset into your thinking

# The authors

Born in 1959, Larry Downes is a consultant with 20 years of experience of working with global businesses. He also teaches law and technology at Northwestern University

Chunka Mui is Executive Editor of the business magazine Context and a Partner with Diamond Technology Partners. He is also Director of the Diamond Exchange, a forum for exploring issues in digital strategy.

## Sources and further reading

Downes, Larry and Mui, Chunka (1998) *Unleashing the Killer App: Digital Strategies for Market Dominance*, Harvard Business School Press.
Downes and Mui have developed a companion Website, which allows budding digital strategists to communicate and share thinking around the globe. Bearing in mind Metcalfe's Law, www.killer-apps.com may in time well grow to be a more vital resource than the book.

# ESTHER DYSON

## *Release 2.1*

## 1998

E sther Dyson has attracted a lot of labels over the years – entrepreneur, high-tech industry analyst, first lady of the Internet, government adviser, queen of the digerati, and Net expert amongst others. She came to fame as the president and owner of Edventures Holdings, and as the driving force behind *Release 1.0*, a respected monthly newsletter for the high-tech industry.

In 1997, Dyson published a book – *Release 2.0* – for which she "re-purposed" and augmented material that featured in her newsletter. *Release 2.1* is her "upgrade" to *Release 2.0*. In her preface to *Release 2.1*, she explains the philosophy behind the name of the book:

> "The very title of this book embodies the concept of flexibility and learning from errors: In the software business, 'Release 1.0' is the first commercial version of a new product, following test versions usually called 0.5, 0.8, 0.9, 0.91, 0.92 ... It's fresh and new, the realization of the hopes and dreams of its developers. It embodies new ideas and it is supposed to be perfect. Usually the vendor comes out with Release 1.1 a few months later, fixing unexpected bugs and tidying up loose ends, many of them pointed out by 'helpful' users.
>
> "If the product succeeds, the vendor launches Release 2.0 a year or so later. Release 2.0 is supposed to be perfect, but usually Release 2.1 comes out a few months after that."

While *Release 1.0* is written for people in the computer business, *Release 2.0* is aimed at a broader audience, one she felt needed an encouraging word rather than a marketing pitch.

Much has happened since the first edition of Dyson's book was published in 1997, and she smoothly incorporates her updates into the

---

**Zeitbite**

"The value of e-commerce is not in the 'e' but in the commerce."
Esther Dyson, writing in *Management Today*, June 2000

---

original manuscript. The most notable changes to the book reflect the growth of e-commerce. Dyson charts the progress of eight companies featured in *2.0*; she also introduces five new Internet businesses. She also assesses many of the tensions that exist around the Internet – for example, between flourishing creativity and the protection of intellectual property, and between government monitoring and personal autonomy. Elsewhere, she takes a look beyond technology to the people who live and work in a technological world, and looks at the changes technology will make to society and its structures. *2.1* also draws on excerpts from e-mails posted to her Website.

The book is clearly written by somebody with an insider's knowledge, and most readers will find it insightful, accessible and pertinent. The main exceptions will be the seasoned Internet users among us who are likely to be familiar with most of the topics on which Dyson gives her commentary.

### Esther Dyson's design rules for living

- *Use your own judgement.* Many newcomers to the Internet are tempted to defer to others, believing them to be better informed and with a deeper understanding of net issues. the Net provides an opportunity for you to take soundings but trust your own views.
- *Disclose yourself.* Let others know what you stand for.
- *Trust but verify.* use the Net to check the credentials of strangers and organizations.
- *Contribute to the communities you love or build your own.* Says Dyson, "There's nothing more satisfying than creating a community in collaboration with others. If you can't find a community to accomplish something you think should happen, design and build your own.
- *Assert your own rights and respect those of others.* Acknowledge the Net's capability for two-way interaction.

- *Don't get into silly fights.* It's easier to walk away from fights on the Net than it is in real life. Bypass the offending person or entity rather than get provoked.
- *Ask questions.* "The Net," says Dyson, "is a great place to ask questions, because you are more likely to be able to find someone who knows the answer.
- *Be a producer.* The real promise of the Net is that is lets you be a producer without all the overhead that used to accompany the production process.
- *Be generous.* This rule is not Net-specific although the Net can often play a part is your being generous and doing small but important favors for others.
- *Have a sense of humor.* "A perfect world would be boring: an imperfect world offer opportunities for humor."
- *Always make new mistakes.* The challenge is not to avoid mistakes, but to learn from them.
- Now design your own rules.

Taken from *Release 2.1*

## The author

Esther Dyson is President and Owner of Edventure Holdings, but is perhaps best know for publishing *Release 1.0*, a monthly newsletter on developments in information technology. She has written articles for the *New York Times*, *Harvard Business Review*, *Wired* and the *Washington Post*. Sister of George Dyson, author of *Darwin among the Machines*, she lives in New York City.

## Sources and further reading

Dyson, Esther (1998) *Release 2.1, a Design for Living in the Digital Age*, Broadway Books, USA.
The Edventure Holdings Website is located at www.edventure.com
Dyson, Esther, (1997) *Release 2.0: a Design for Living in the Digital Age*, Broadway Books, USA.

# PHILIP EVANS & THOMAS WURSTER

## *Blown to Bits*

### 2000

T hose of us in the business of communicating information to others have until now faced a strategic choice, which can be characterized as richness or reach. Providing rich, customized information about a product or service necessarily limited the number of potential customers that could be reached with that information. On the other hand, going for reach necessarily meant the degree of customization of the information reduced in direct correlation with the widening universe of customers. So, which to go for? This simple yet absolute trade-off has long stood at the center of the information business.

Indeed, the organization providing the information itself reflects a trade-off between richness and reach – essentially providing, a physical infrastructure and established behavioral patterns that enable and govern the sharing of information vital to the work of business.

According to Philip Evans and Thomas S. Wurster, two consultants from the Boston Consulting Group, this dilemma is fast disappearing as advanced digital technologies are allowing information to separate from its physical carrier. This, in effect, kills off the richness/reach trade-off and renders many traditional business structures and the strategies that drive them obsolete.

They begin *Blown to Bits* with a case study showing how Microsoft's Encarta blew Encyclopaedia Britannica out of the water. The multi-volume version of the prestigious Britannica dominated the encyclopaedia market for most of the 20th century, with sales reaching a peak of $650 million in 1990. The marketing proposition – educational advantage for your kids at a price – was compelling and successful. Since 1990, sales of printed encyclopaedias have plummeted by 80%, "blown away by a product of the late twentieth century information revolution: the CD-ROM."

There are other examples of what the authors call "the new economics of information." In the music industry right now, we can witness a lively ongoing struggle around MP3 and related technologies.

This is not just a matter of concern for those working in explicit "information" businesses. The authors argue that in every industry information is the "glue" that holds value chains, supply chains, consumer franchises, and organizations together across the entire economy, and go on to illustrate how the melting of this glue has major implications. They describe how the explosion in connectivity and the adoption of common information standards are causing the blow-up of the richness/reach trade-off and radically transforming economic relationships in all their manifestations. A sales force, a system of branches, a printing press, a chain of stores, or a delivery fleet – which once served as formidable barriers to entry because they took years and heavy investment to build – suddenly become expensive liabilities. As the informational glue that holds these structures together begins to melt, pieces of the business will break apart and recombine in entirely new ways. Insurgent players, newly armed with the ability to provide both richness and reach to customers – and unburdened by cumbersome physical assets – will emerge from nowhere to pick off the most profitable slivers within scores of industries.

This will engender a process of deconstruction, involving the breaking apart and recombining of traditional business structures. The bad news, say the authors, is that deconstruction is most likely to strike in exactly the area of the business an incumbent can least afford to lose. They go on to explain how leaders can assess the vulnerability of their own businesses and respond. They also describe how a new form of disintermediation, driven by the new economics of information, threatens not just to re-segment markets, but to destroy the intermediary business model entirely.

One of the most dramatic aspects of deconstruction, say the authors, will be the rise of navigators as independent businesses. They maintain that today's new electronic retailers and navigators will prove as powerful and aggressive as today's category-killing retailers, and describe how the competitive battlefield will be fought across three dimensions: *reach, affiliation, and richness.* In detailing how the new world of navigation will evolve, the authors underscore the importance of achieving, critical mass, explain how the critical shift in affiliation from the seller to the customer will occur, explain various richness strategies based on both product and customer-specific information, and forecast the likely winners and losers.

*Blown to Bits* is a compelling mix of strategic analysis and practical guidance. The authors' analysis is convincing, and it really does appear as though the only options available in the new economics of information are to use the "un-gluing" of industries to establish a competitive advantage. The alternative is simply to fall apart at the seams.

### Reality check: no, we're not in denial

In an interview with Amazon.co.uk, Philip Evans explains how business people get, but don't get, the new economics of information:

*Amazon.co.uk:* How do most businesspeople respond when you tell them their businesses are about to come unglued?

*Evans:* I do a lot of speaking, and about a year ago, I gave two speeches in the same week. One was to a group of newspaper executives and the other was to a group of bankers. And I made the Blown to Bits argument for the newspaper audience by talking about banking, and they all agreed. And then, when I said, "Well, of course, you do realize the same logic applies to you," they all vigorously disagreed – said that was absolute nonsense. And then, a few days later, talking to the banking audience, I made the argument by using the newspaper industry, and they all agreed: "Yes, it's obviously true." And yet, when I said, "Well, it applies to you, too," they all similarly said, "No, that's absolute nonsense." So while everybody can see the logic in other businesses, it's much harder for them to see it in their own. But I can't help noticing that more recently people have begun to accept that this change is cutting much closer to the core of their business identities than they ever thought.

## *The authors*

Philip Evans is a senior vice president of The Boston Consulting Group in Boston. He can be reached at evans.philip@bcg.com. Thomas S. Wurster is a Senior Vice President of The Boston Consulting Group in Los Angeles. He can be reached at wurster.tom@bcg.com. Evans and Wurster are co-leaders of The Boston Consulting Group's Media and Convergence Practice.

## Sources and further reading

Evans, Philip, and Wurster, Thomas S (2000) *Blown to Bits: How the New Economics of Information Transforms Strategy*, Harvard Business School Press, USA.

Evans, Philip, and Wurster, Thomas S. (1999), Getting real about virtual commerce, *Harvard Business Review*, November–December.

Evans, Philip, and Wurster, Thomas S. (1999), Strategy and the new economics of information, *Harvard Business Review*, September–October.

# CHARLES FERGUSON

## *High Stakes, No Prisoners*

### 1999

I n 1994, Charles Ferguson – consultant, writer and holder of a PhD from the Massachusetts Institute of Technology – set up a company called Vermeer Technologies, named after his favorite painter. It was not the easiest of times to launch a startup in Silicon Valley, with the US emerging gingerly from a recession, a flat stock market, and the Internet yet to be taken seriously by those with money to invest. Yet within two years he sold the company to Microsoft for $133 million, in the process making a fortune for himself and his associates.

Vermeer's "very cool, very big idea" was FrontPage, the first software product for creating and managing a Website, which is now bundled with Microsoft Office and boasts several million users worldwide.

Cue another self-congratulatory business book about how somebody made their millions on the market? Actually no. *High Stakes, No Prisoners* gives a "warts and all" view into the inner workings of Silicon Valley. In one of his most memorable lines, he describes it as a place where "one finds little evidence that the meek shall inherit the earth."

Ferguson is unerringly candid throughout the book, naming names of the people he came across – many of them big movers and the shakers in the industry – and saying what he really thinks of them. For example, he describes Netscape CEO Jim Barksdale as having a poor technical grasp, being "in over his head from day one" at Netscape, yet at the same time displaying "extraordinary arrogance." Oracle founder Larry Ellison is "a notorious womanizer – and a seriously random number."

Ferguson is very tough on himself, too, owning up to the mistakes his start-up made, and detailing his own shortcomings as a person and a businessman. There can't be many business books around where the index lists, under the heading of the author's name, "mistakes of," "naïveté of," and "paranoia of."

Best of all, *High Stakes, No Prisoners* is an honest, acerbic and extremely funny account of how business really gets done in high technology. For instance, here's Ferguson on doing a start-up:

> "Startups are the intellectual equivalent of driving a small, fast convertible with the top down, the stereo playing Keith Jarrett, Bach, or J.J. Cale very loud, doing a hundred miles an hour on an empty road at sunset. You might crash, but the experience is visceral, immediate, and intense."

On venture capitalists:

> "Andy Marcuvitz is a heavyset guy who wears badly fitting suits. He has no discernible personality, sense of humor, or compassion – ideal traits for a venture capitalist."

Taking Vermeer from inception to its sale to Microsoft was, he writes, "an amazing experience" but he concludes his book by admitting that he thinks "it will be a while before I run another company again." Let's hope that it won't be too long before he turns his caustic pen to a subject that is equally fascinating, and to which he can bring just as much insight and humor.

## Vermeer: from zero to hero

In a ten-week period beginning in early September of 1995, Vermeer Technologies went from being an unknown development-phase company to being the hottest, coolest start-up in the United States. In part due to this change, but also for other reasons, my life simultaneously went from being demanding but manageable to being completely, totally insane. September through Christmas 1995 would prove to be the most exciting yet punishing months of my professional life.

One year earlier, we'd had to fight for months to raise $4 million. Even in March, when we had tried to counter NaviSoft's product launch, nobody had paid us the slightest attention. But by the end of September, we had the opposite problem, and it was a very serious problem indeed. Everyone either wanted a piece of our hide or they wanted us dead because we threatened them. And my problems were by no means confined to the outside world. To the contrary, I needed to defend both Vermeer and myself against our investors and our newly hired CEO just as much as against external threats. Events were moving at the speed of light, everything was connected to everything else, and there was essentially nobody I could talk to about it. So these developments brought astonishing highs and great personal fulfillment, but also brutal fights, extreme stress, and painful lessons.

Even through August, we had been quite secretive. While we had been speaking to potential partners, large customers, and analysts, we did so very selectively, under nondisclosure, and usually without revealing sensitive technology or strategic plans. But by September our product was nearly done, and it was time to announce ourselves to the world. Our timing was perfect; as we had planned, we could launch in the peak of the fall season. We wanted business, and there was no further point in concealing what either we or our product did. Furthermore, it was also time to raise more money. So it was time to show our stuff. When we did the response was, as they say, overwhelming.

So when Peter Amstein and I arrived at the room we'd been assigned for our presentation at Dick Shaffer's Digital Media Outlook conference on September 11, 1995, we found the place packed and the atmosphere electric. Every seat and every square inch was occupied. Venture capitalists, investment bankers, technology executives, and industry gurus were lined up along the walls, with more straining to hear from the doorway and the corridor outside. Everyone had already heard of us, but none of them had ever seen our presentations or software before. They liked what they saw. Afterward we were surrounded by people shoving cards at us, wanting meetings, asking if we were raising money, inviting us to conferences, offering partnerships.

## The author

Charles Ferguson consulted to the White House, many agencies of the US government, and some of the world's leading high-tech companies before founding Vermeer Technologies with Randy Forgaard in 1993. He has contributed to *Harvard Business Review*, the *New York Times*, and *Foreign Policy*. He holds a PhD in political science from Massachusetts of Technology. He can be reached by e-mail at charles@highstakesnoprisoners.com.

## Sources and further reading

Ferguson, Charles H. (1999) *High Stakes, No Prisoners: a Winner's Tale of Greed and Glory in the Internet Wars*, Times Business, USA.

Ferguson, Charles H. & Morris, Charles (1993) *Computer Wars*, Times Business, USA.
The authors suggest that the power shift from IBM to Microsoft – the consequences of IBM failing to exploit its own inventions and the importance of becoming the industry standard setter – had more to do with IBM committing a series of blunders than with Microsoft doing anything exceptional.

# FRANCIS FUKUYAMA

## *Trust*

## 1995

M ost commentators agree that globalization is having a direct, and to a degree, homogenizing impact on countries, both economically and politically. But what about culturally? Francis Fukuyama is not convinced: on a cultural level, he maintains, it's not nearly as clear that homogenization is proceeding nearly as rapidly. If anything, he says he detects a distinct resistance to cultural homogenization.

This is important, he says, when considering the roots of economic behavior and the determinants of national economic success because culture is of critical importance to everyday economic life.

Following this premise a step further, if a national culture has some kind of impact on national economic behavior, what is at the heart of national culture? Fukuyama believes that the level of trust present in a society is the key, performance-determining, aspect of national culture and that only those societies with a high degree of social trust will be able to create the flexible large scale business organizations that are needed to compete in the new global economy.

In *Trust: the Social Virtues and the Creation of Prosperity*, Fukuyama describes three types of trust: the first based on the family, the second revolves around voluntary associations beyond the family, and the third concerns the state. Each of the three categories has a corresponding organizational form; the family business, the professionally managed corporation and the state-owned enterprise, respectively.

In countries where family ties are strong (and trust of those outside the family correspondingly weak), people tend to look to the state to create the large professionally managed corporations. Societies with high levels of trust seem to be capable of creating large economic organizations without state support. Fukuyama cites China, South Korea, Italy, and France as low trust societies with a strong role for the family and weak associations outside the family group. In contrast, he claims, Japan, the United States, and Germany are high trust societies with strong and plentiful associations beyond the family.

For societies to be economically competitive at a global level, they need to extend what Fukuyama calls their "radius of trust" so that trust is embodied in the institutions of society. This bodes well for northern Europe and the US, but is less good news for countries where levels of trust are low.

Interestingly, the East Asian tigers economies were enjoying unhampered economic growth in the mid-nineties when *Trust* was published, despite being rated by Fukuyama as low trust societies. Their subsequent fall from grace seems to lend some weight to Fukuyama's hypothesis.

That said, he does not go so far as to make an absolute case for cultural determinism. He does not believe that certain societies are bound to succeed while others falter. He writes that "there is no necessary trade-off between community and efficiency"; although he continues, "…but those who pay attention to community may indeed become the most efficient of all."

Some have criticized Fukuyama for being too reductionist in his line of argument, including examples which fit his needs while ignoring counter-examples which could undermine his overall stance. Readers will need to make up their own minds, but in an era when social capital may be as important as physical capital, Fukuyama's study of the interconnectedness of economic life with cultural life makes necessary reading.

### Reality check

And conversely, we are constantly confronted by Western ideologists – Mr. Fukuyama, the Doctor Pangloss of the 1990s, comes to mind – for whom the rich world's superiority simply expresses its discovery of the best of all possible designs for arranging human affairs, as demonstrated by its historic triumph. In simpler words, these ideologists have the conviction that Westerners know better – which is far from self-evident. As the tragic record of Western economic advisers in post-Soviet Russia shows, it may be difficult for intelligent and well-intentioned academics and consultants even to grasp what is happening in environments so different from their own, and shaped by such different histories and cultures.

Indeed, in a world filled with such inequalities, to live in the favored regions is to be virtually cut off from the experience, let alone the reactions, of people outside those regions. It takes an enormous effort of the imagination, as well as a great deal of knowledge, to break out of our comfortable, protected, and self-absorbed enclaves and enter an uncomfortable and unprotected larger world inhabited by the majority of the human species.

Source: Eric Hobsbawm (2000) *The New Century*,
Little, Brown, UK.

## The author

Francis Fukuyama is a former deputy director of the US State Department's policy planning staff. He is now an analyst at the RAND corporation. He is author of *The End of History and the Last Man* (Hamish Hamilton, 1992), which explored the way in which different countries were adopting increasingly similar political and economic institutions.

## Sources and further reading

Fukuyama, Francis (1995) *Trust: the Social Virtues and the Creation of Prosperity*, Hamish Hamilton, UK.

Fukuyama, Francis (1999) *The Great Disruption: Human Nature and the Reconstitution of Social Order*, Profile Books, UK.
Another big-think book, this time on social order and human nature. The "great disruption" Fukuyama refers to is the transition from the industrial to the information society. He argues that humankind is driven biologically to create new forms of social order.

# BILL GATES

## *Business @ the Speed of Thought*

1999

## Three news stories

### *Beyond dot.coms and beyond browsing*

On 22nd June 2000, Microsoft announced a strategy designed to move its business away from the personal computer base that the company has embraced since the mid-1970s. Gates described Microsoft.Net, an approach to computing the company once scoffed at, as the most significant initiative in the company's history, saying it would reshape Microsoft's business and fundamentally change the way computers are used. At the heart of the plan is Windows.Net, a new version of the Windows operating system that will, for example, enable users to edit, filter and personalize the content of Web pages.

Source: *Financial Times*, June 23, 2000

### *Judge Sends Microsoft Appeal to Supreme Court*

On 20th June 2000, the trial judge in the Microsoft antitrust case has issued a surprise order this evening, delaying the sweeping conduct restrictions he had imposed on the company until a higher court acts. Until the order by the judge, the Supreme Court would have been called on to rule quickly on Microsoft's request to stay the remedy order. Now the Supreme Court, or the appeals court, can review the entire appeal, and rule on it, before deciding whether to impose the judge's remedy, modify it or cancel it. The process could take a year or longer.

Source: *New York Times*, June 21, 2000

### Fearful of Microsoft, China Backs Linux

Chinese leaders are concerned that the country is growing overly dependent on the Windows operating system. But the Chinese government, itself a master at monopoly, is taking its case not to the courtroom but to the marketplace. It is backing Linux.

Source: *New York Times*, July 8, 2000.

These three stories, all decently significant, were culled from newspapers over a random two-week period. Whether you love or loathe Bill Gates, whether you admire or despair of Microsoft, there's no doubt that Gates and his company are significant global players. Antitrust hearings aside, what Gates says will happen in the world of technology has more than a fair chance of coming to pass.

This reason alone explains the inclusion of *Business @ the Speed of Thought*, in which Gates uses case studies from around the world to demonstrate the transformative power of technology in business. Beyond that, he provides the reader with his view on technology's role in corporate evolution – not just for rival corporate giants but for small businesses as well.

*Business @ the Speed of Thought* also explores the concept of the digital nervous system, a system that unites all systems and processes under one common infrastructure. Gates describes a digital nervous system as "the corporate, digital equivalent of the human nervous system, providing a well-integrated flow of information to the right part of the organization at the right time. A digital nervous system consists of the digital processes that enable a company to perceive and react to its environment, to sense competitor challenges and customer needs, and to organize timely responses. A digital nervous system requires a combination of hardware and software; it's distinguished from a mere network of computers by the accuracy, immediacy, and richness of the information it brings to knowledge workers and the *insight and collaboration* made possible by the information."

He goes on to explain how such a system might be put in place and describes some of the pitfalls to be avoided.

In truth, *Business @ the Speed of Thought* is not a great book (and coming in at around 500 pages, it's certainly not a concise book). Because Gates has a world view that puts the technology itself in pole position, we don't really get any consideration of the new economy's wider issues. This is a book by a techno-enthusiast aimed at others for whom the technology is all important. And even judged by those standards, this is not a particularly rounded view of the technology scene. There is a sense of "If Microsoft aren't doing it, it's not worth talking about" here. So Gates is not the person to read if you want to know more about Linux, reckoned by many to be a better operating system than Microsoft's, and available free on the Internet.

The book also has a limited shelf life. *Business @ the Speed of Thought* will probably date as quickly as Gates' previous book *The Road Ahead*, which came out in 1995. To prove that Bill's crystal ball is just as foggy as everybody else's, *The Road Ahead* devoted only 20 pages to the topic of the Internet.

So when the second edition of *Writing the New Economy* comes along, don't expect *Business @ the Speed of Thought* to feature in it. On the other hand, there may well be a new Gates book on the market by then, and it would be unwise – barring a spectacular fall from grace by Gates – to bank against its inclusion. Chances are, when Bill speaks, the world will still need to pay attention.

## Reality check

"We do not have to choose between unfettered info-global capitalism and communal retrenchment. New information technologies (including ethically controlled genetic engineering) could yield their promise of a virtuous interaction between the power of mind and the well-being of society. No need to look into the future: just look around at courageous efforts such as those taking place in Finland. The Finns have quietly established themselves as the first true information society, with one Website per person, Internet access in 100 percent of schools, a computer literacy campaign for adults, the largest diffusion of computer power and mobile telephony in the world, and a globally competitive information technology industry, spearheaded by Nokia. At the same time they have kept in place, with some fine-tuning, the welfare state. Finnish society fosters citizen participation and safeguards civility. It is probably not an accident that Linus Torvalds is a Finn. Torvalds is the software innovator who, as a 21-year-old student at the University of Helsinki, created Linux, a much better operating system than Microsoft's, and released it free on the Internet. By so doing, he contributed to a growing open access software code movement, with thousands of Linux users contributing online to improve the code. Its users – currently about ten million – consider it far superior to any other Unix software, precisely because it is continuously improved by the work of their collective mind. Open information technology contributes to much better information technology, empowering minds around the world to use technology for living. That includes making money, without equating their lives to their stocks.

"The catch is that Linus Torvalds now lives in Silicon Valley."
Source: Manuel Castells, from an essay featured in Will Hutton & Anthony Giddens (2000) *On the Edge*, Jonathan Cape.

## The author

Bill Gates is Chairman of Microsoft, the company he co-founded with Paul Allen in 1975.

## Sources and further reading

Gates, William H. (1999) *Business @ the Speed of Thought*, Warner Books, USA.
There is an associated Website located at www.Speed-of-Thought.com
Gates, William H (1995) *The Road Ahead*, Warner Books, USA.

# WILLIAM GIBSON

## *Neuromancer*

## 1984

"Cyberspace. A consensual hallucination experienced daily by billions of legitimate operators, in every nation, by children being taught mathematical concepts ... A graphic representation of data abstracted from the banks of every computer in the human system. Unthinkable complexity. Lines of light arranged in the non-space of the mind, clusters and constellations of data. Like city lights receding ..."

yberspace. A key concept in *Neuromancer*, William Gibson's dark, powerful and astonishingly prescient science fiction novel, that won the Hugo Award, the Nebula Award and the Philip K Dick Memorial award.

Kevin Kelly, in his book *Out of Control* offers this brilliant encapsulation of cyberspace as originally envisioned by Gibson:

"Cyberspace encompasses the realm of large electronic networks which are invisibly spreading 'underneath' the industrial world in a kind of virtual sprawl. In the near future, according to Gibson's science-fiction, cyberspace explorers would 'jack in' to a borderless maze of electronic data banks and video-gamelike worlds. A cyberspace scout sits in a dark room and then plugs a modem directly into his brain. Thus jacked in, he cerebrally navigates the invisible world of abstracted information, as if he were racing through an infinite library ... Cyberspace, as expanded by hippie mystic Barlow, is something yet broader. It includes not only the invisible matrix of databases and networks, and not only the three-dimensional games one can enter wearing computer-screen goggles, but also the entire realm of any disembodied presence and of all information in digital form. Cyberspace, says Barlow, is the place that you and a friend 'are' when you are both talking on the phone. 'Nothing could be more disembodied than cyberspace. It's like having your everything amputated,' Barlow once told a reporter. Cyberspace is the mall of network culture. It's that territory where the counterintuitive logic of distributed networks meets the odd behavior of human society. And it is expanding rapidly. Because of network economics, cyberspace is a resource that increases the more it is used."

It is Gibson's depiction of a fully connected world and his exploration of the concept of the idea of virtual reality that earn him his place as a new economy visionary.

As to the plot of *Neuromancer*, it is based around an attempt to hack into a mainframe where an Artificial Intelligence resides. Gibson's characters – notably Case, a burnt out software cowboy – are well drawn and engage our interest. Gibson writes extremely well, avoiding the over-descriptive verbosity that afflict many sci-fi writers. and leaving a satisfying resonance in the mind. However, if you can't stand the thought of picking up a science fiction book, the good news is that *Neuromancer* is less required reading and more a book to shamelessly namedrop in the presence of impressionable colleagues.

## The author

William Gibson lives in Vancouver, Canada. His most recent book, *All Tomorrow's Parties*, published in 1999, reintroduces characters from *Virtual Light* and *Idoru* to complete a stunningly imagined trilogy

## Sources and further reading

Gibson, William (1984) *Neuromancer*, HarperCollins, USA.

### Two more novels for the new economy

Douglas Coupland
*Microserfs*
Flamingo, 1995
In *Microserfs*, Coupland, author of *Generation X*, introduces us to

Dan, a programmer at Microsoft, who shares a house with five other Microsoft employees. Presented in the form of Dan's journal, the book recounts how the six of them struggle to get a life while working within a high-speed corporate environment. Coupland never reveals his cards too obviously, preferring to let his thoughts on technology, work and myriad other topics emerge through dialogue, anecdotes, and asides.

For example, Dan regularly checks the Microsoft share price: "The stock closed up $1.75 on Friday. Bill has 78,000,000 shares so that means he's now $136.5 million richer. I have almost no stock, and this means I'm a loser."

Another line: "Speaking of the information superhighway, we have all given each other official permission to administer a beating to whoever uses that accursed term. We're so sick of it!"

And another: "Learned a new word today. 'Interiority' – it means, *being inside somebody's head.*"

Quirky, humorous, and actually quite touching in places, *Microserfs* remains Coupland's finest achievement to date.

*The Author:* Douglas Coupland was born in 1961 on a Canadian NATO base in Germany. He grew up in Vancouver, Canada, where he still lives.

Neal Stephenson
*Snow Crash*
Bantam Books, USA, 1992
Freelance hacker, samurai swordsman and pizza delivery boy Hiro Protagonist and business partner YT (short for Yours Truly) attempt to save the world from linguistic devastation, religious fanaticism, software viruses, a cyber-librarian, a robotic dog and the Mob. A fast, funny and challenging read which describes text-free cyberspace communities, anticipating the possibility that the written word might fade as the primary form of discourse.

*The Author:* Neal Stephenson has published five novels. The most recent, *Cryptonomicon*, was published in 1999.

# ANDREW GROVE

## *Only the Paranoid Survive*

### 1996

O nce dubbed "the best manager in the world" by *Fortune* magazine, Andy Grove is also one of the world's best-known business figures. A co-founder of Intel in 1979, he helped the
company grow into what it is today – the world's largest
computer chipmaker, not to mention the fifth most admired company
in America and the seventh most profitable company among the *Fortune*
500.

Given his substantial managerial achievements at Intel, it would not
have been all that surprising if he had produced a book to add to that
already over-crowded genre, the self-aggrandizing CEO autobiography.
In fact, he is relatively restrained in his use of Intel to illustrate his
themes, and when he does it is more often than not to admit to tactical
and strategic mistakes made by the company.

Grove has bigger fish to fry. *Only the Paranoid Survive* is a lesson in
leadership and strategy that could benefit any manager in any industry.
Grove provides a lens through which to view the challenges posed by an
ever-changing business environment, and offers a set of strategic tools to
help managers recognize and successfully address those changes.

His start-point is the best known and most influential classical
strategy analysis model of all – Michael Porter's Five Competitive Forces
– which he paraphrases and augments to produce his own version.
Grove's six forces affecting a business are:

1   Power, vigor and competence of existing competitors.
2   Power, vigor and competence of complementors.
3   Power, vigor and competence of customers.
4   Power, vigor and competence of suppliers.
5   Power, vigor and competence of potential competitors.

6    Possibility that what your business is doing can be done in a different way.

"Complementors" are Grove's addition to Porter's original model. These are businesses from whom customers buy complementary products e.g. computers need software, software needs computers. He calls complementors "fellow travelers." In Intel's case, their most significant complementor is Microsoft, which helps explain Grove's vocal support for Bill Gates during the Antitrust hearings.

Groves cites the sixth force, termed "substitution" by Porter, as "the most deadly of all" because "new techniques, new approaches, new technologies can upset the old order, mandate a new set of rules and create an entirely new climate in which to do business."

A linked concept is what he calls a "10X factor," "When a Wal-mart moves into a small town," he writes, " the environment changes for every retailer in that town. A '10X' factor has arrived. When the technology for sound in movies became popular, every silent actor and actress personally experiences the "10X" factor of technological change."

A "10X factor" brings massive change into the dynamics of an industry. Examples include the first on-line bank, Amazon's entry into the book market, and the mobile phone.

If "10X" factors are the drivers of massive change, strategic inflection points (SIPS) are those moments in the life history of a business when such change occurs. During an SIP, Grove writes, the way a business operates, the very structure and concept of the business, undergoes a change. But the irony is that at that point itself nothing much happens. That subtle point is like the eye of the hurricane ... when it moves the wind hits you again. That is what happens in the middle of the transformation from one business model to another."

SIPs are his "big idea" (such that his original title for the book was *Strategic Inflection Points* until his publishers stepped in within the much more arresting *Only the Paranoid Survive*) and in a business world that he characterizes as "jungle law" they are a vital tool in helping companies scan the horizon for seismic changes that can rewrite industry rules.

SIPs are not limited to high-tech industries like Intel, but are particularly prevalent in the new economy. And the Internet may just be the biggest SIP of all. Grove believes that within five years "all companies will be Internet companies or they won't be companies at all. In other words, companies not using the Internet to improve just about every facet of their business operation will be destroyed by competitors who do."

Although Grove is one of life's techno-determinists, it's becoming increasing difficult to quibble with this assessment. What is exciting and disquieting in equal measure is the thought that, as far as the Internet is concerned, we are still in the hurricane's eye.

### Reality check: Andy Grove on strategic inflection points

An inflection point occurs where the old strategic picture dissolves and gives way to the new, allowing the business to ascend to new heights. However, if you don't navigate your way through an inflection point, you go through a peak and after the peak the business declines. Put another way, before the strategic inflection point, the industry simply was more like the old. After it, it is more like the new.

So how do we know that a set of circumstances is a strategic inflection point?

Most of the time, recognition takes place in stages.

First, there is a troubling sense that something is different. Things don't work the way they used to. Customers' attitudes toward you are different. Competitors that you wrote off or hardly knew existed are stealing business from you.

Then there is a growing dissonance between what your company thinks it is doing and what is actually happening inside the bowels of the organization. Such misalignment between corporate statements and operational actions hints at more than the normal chaos that you have learned to live with.

Eventually, a new framework, a new set of understandings, a new set of actions emerges. It's as if the group that was lost finds its bearings again. (This could take a year – or a decade.) Last of all, a new set of corporate statements is generated, often by a new set of senior managers.

Given the amorphous nature of an inflection point, how do you know the right moment to take appropriate action, to make the changes that will save your company or your career? Unfortunately, you don't.

But you can't wait until you do know: Timing is everything. If you undertake these changes while your company is still healthy, you can save much more of your company's strength, your employees and your strategic position. But that means acting when not everything is known, when the data aren't yet in. Even those who believe in a scientific approach to management will have to rely on instinct and personal judgement. When you're caught in the turbulence of a strategic inflection point, the sad fact is that instinct and judgement are all you've got to guide you through.

But the good news is that even though your judgement got you into this tough position, it can also get you out. It's just a question of training your instincts to pick up a different set of signals. These signals may have been out there all along but you may have ignored them. The strategic inflection point is the time to wake up and listen.

An edited extract from *Only the Paranoid Survive*

## The author

Born in Hungary in 1936, Andy Grove emigrated to the US in 1956. After graduating with a PhD from the University of California at Berkeley, he joined the Fairchild Semiconductor Corp., before co-founding Intel in 1979.

He stepped down as CEO of Intel in 1998, but continues as Chairman of the Board.

## Sources and further reading

Grove, Andrew S. (1996) *Only the Paranoid Survive: How to Exploit the Crisis Points that Challenge Every Company and Career*, HarperBusiness, USA.

Jackson, Tim (1997) *Inside Intel*, HarperCollins, USA.
A less flattering picture of Grove and Intel by a British journalist.

Porter, Michael (1980) *Competitive Strategy*, Free Press, USA.

# CHARLES HANDY

## *The Age of Unreason*

### 1989

**I**n *The Age of Unreason,* Charles Handy tells us a story to demonstrate the nature of discontinuous change:

"Thirty years ago I started work in a world-famous multinational company. By way of encouragement they produced an outline of my future career. 'This will be your life,' they said, 'with titles of likely jobs.' The line ended, I remember, with myself as Chief Executive of a particular company in a particular far-off country. I was, at the time, suitably flattered. I left them long before I reached the heights they planned for me, but I already knew that not only did the job they had picked out no longer exist, neither did the company I would have directed, nor even the country in which I was to have operated."

The story nicely illustrates Handy's style – conversational, anecdotal and open. It also sums up what he means by the age of unreason: it's a time "when the future, in so many areas, is to be shaped by us and for us; a time when the only prediction that will hold true is that no predictions will hold true; a time therefore for bold imaginings ... for thinking the unlikely and doing the unreasonable."

Handy goes on to describe three organizational forms that will emerge in an age of unreason:

1  *The shamrock organization.* "A form of organization based around a core of essential executives and workers supported by outside contractors and part-time help."

2  *The federal organization.* A form of decentralized set-up in which the center's powers are given to it by the outlying groups; the center

therefore co-ordinates, advises, influences and suggests rather than directs or controls. Federalism, says Handy, is the way to combine the autonomy of individual parts with the economics of co-ordination.

3   *The Triple I organization.* The three "Is" are Information, Intelligence and Ideas. This type of organization says Handy will resemble a university and will seek to make "added value out of knowledge." To achieve this end, this type of organization "increasingly uses smart machines, with smart people to work with them."

Not only was Handy remarkably prescient in anticipating the growth of outsourcing, telecommuting, the intellectual capital movement, and the rise of knowledge workers *inter alia*, he also foresaw how these developments might impact on the individual. It was his concept of the portfolio worker that arguably provided a way forward for that part of the whole downshifting movement of the nineties that was wrestling with redefining the nature of work as well as questions of life balance.

*The Age of Unreason* reveals Handy at the peak of his powers as a management thinker. In later books and articles, he would increasingly assume the mantle of a social philosopher

## Portfolio working

A work portfolio is a way of describing how the different bits of work in our life fit together to form a balanced whole. "Flat people" as E.M. Forster called them, were those who had only one dimension to their lives. He preferred rounded people. I would now call them portfolio people, the sort of people who, when you ask them what they do, reply, "It will take a while to tell you it all, which bit would you like?" Sooner or later, thanks to the re-shaping of the organization we shall all be portfolio people. It is good news.

### The categories of the portfolio

There are five main categories of work for the Portfolio: *wage work* and *fee work*, which are both forms of paid work; *homework, gift work* and *study work*, which are all free work. The definitions and the differences are obvious but important – the most important being the difference between paid work and free work. It is free work which has been the missing part of the portfolio in recent times.

**Zeitbite**

"Organizations were dreadful places in some ways, but they were places where companionship could be found. We will miss a lot of what organizations used to offer, the familiar faces we liked and the people we hated, the canteen and the gossip. Now we interact only with clients or our competitors. I think we have to have an alternative community of some sort, where we can refresh ourselves and relax. Because loneliness is to me one of the great sadnesses of portfolio life."

Charles Handy, *The Search for Meaning*

- Wage (or salary) work represents money paid for time given. Fee work is money paid for results delivered. Employees do wage work; professionals, craftspeople and freelancers do fee work. Fee work is increasing as jobs move outside the organization. Even some insiders now get fees (bonuses) as well as wages.
- Homework includes that whole catalogue of tasks that go on in the home, from cooking and cleaning, to children and cleaning, from carpentry to chipping. Done willingly or grudgingly, it is all work.
- Gift work is work done for free outside the home, for charities and local groups, for neighbors or for the community.
- Study work done seriously and not frivolously is, to me, a form of work not recreation. Training for a sport or a skill is study work, so is the learning of a new language or a new culture, so are the long days I spend reading other peoples' books in preparation for writing my own.

In the past, for most of us, our work portfolio has had only one item in it, at least for men. It was their job or, more grandiosely, their career. This was, when you think about it, a risky strategy. Few would these days put all their money into one asset, yet that is what a lot of us have been doing with our lives. That one asset, that one job, has had to work overtime for we have looked to it for so many things at once – for interest or satisfaction in the work itself, for interesting people and good company, for security and money, for the chance of development and reality.

---

**Zeitbite**

"It's obviously going to be a different kind of world in the next century ... It will be a world of fleas and elephants, of large conglomerates and small individual entities, of large political and economic blocs and small countries. The smart thing is to be the flea on the back of the elephant. Think of Ireland and the EU, or consultants and the BBC.

"A flea can be global as easily as one of the elephants but can more easily be swept away. Elephants are a guarantee of continuity but fleas provide the innovation. There will also be *ad hoc* organizations, temporary alliances of fleas and elephants to deliver a particular project."

Charles Handy, writing in the October 1999 edition of *CBI News*

---

## Where will the money come from?

That is always the central issue in planning a portfolio. Portfolio people think portfolio money not salary money. They learn that money comes in fits and starts from different sources. There may be a bit of a pension, some part-time work, some fees to charge or things to sell.

- They lead cash-flow lives not salary lives, planning always to have enough in-flows to cover out-flows.
- Portfolio people even like paying VAT, it gives them on average two months' free money from the Government.
- Portfolio people think in terms of barter. They exchange houses for holidays, baby-sit for each other, lend garden tools in return for produce, give free lodging in return for secretarial help in the evenings.
- Portfolio people know that most skills are saleable if you want to sell them. If you love designing houses, design someone else's; if you like photographing dogs, photograph other people's dogs; if you like driving, drive other people's errands – and charge a fee if you need money. Hobbies can be mini-businesses for portfolio people – cooking can be their skill, plants their merchandise.
- Portfolios accumulate by chance. They should accumulate by choice. We can manage our time. We can say no. We can give less priority, or more, to homework or to paid work. Money is essential but more money is not always essential. Enough can be enough.

Derived from *The Age of Unreason* by Charles Handy

## The author

Charles Handy is a writer, lecturer, broadcaster, and self-styled social philosopher. He divides his time between living and working in London and his rural retreat in Norfolk.

## Sources and further reading

Handy, Charles (1989) *The Age of Unreason*, Hutchinson, UK.

Handy, Charles (1999) *The New Alchemists*, Hutchinson, UK.
At the heart of *The New Alchemists* is a series of interviews with 29 people who have made something out of nothing in either the business or arts worlds, or for the community. Those featured include inventor Trevor Baylis (creator of the clockwork radio), Andy Law of the St Luke's ad agency, Geoff Mulgan (founder of Demos), Tim Waterstone of the eponymous bookshop, BA's Bob Ayling (whose inclusion seems open to question to be honest) and the UK's Master Alchemist Richard Branson. And what makes an Alchemist? According to Handy, they have three overriding qualities:

- *Dedication:* caring passionately about what they are trying to bring into being.
- *Doggedness:* a wholehearted commitment to achieving results through hard work, determination, and tenacity.
- *Difference:* a mixture of personality and talent that leads Alchemists to do things differently or to do different things.

This level of analysis is fine as far as it goes but unfortunately Handy doesn't seem to go much deeper. Although the book itself is over 250 pages long, the individual profiles rarely surpass *Hello* magazine level in depth or insight (each profile is typically five pages in length, including two pages of photographs by Handy's wife Elizabeth). This lack of incisiveness is never really resolved, as can be seen from the book's final summarizing paragraph:

> "There is much that we don't know about alchemy, even after a concentrated year of talking to some outstanding practitioners. They themselves do not find it easy to explain – how do you make it clear the way to ride a bicycle to someone who has

never been on one? Those who know it can only demonstrate, not elucidate. Which is why there are some unanswered questions and why, in the end, we can only learn by watching others and imitate, practise and make it our own. The best that we, the authors, can do is to make it fashionable to try, for fashion is still one of the most powerful agents of change in every field, including that of business and social organizations."

This level of analysis just isn't good enough for somebody who is the UK's only authentic management guru.

At one level, *The New Alchemists* would grace any managerial bookshelf – it is beautifully designed and it takes on a genuinely interesting topic. However, having read it from cover to cover, this reader is left with the overriding impression that Handy has produced the first business coffee table book when he should have been using the same material to write the *Harvard Business Review* article of the year.

Handy, Charles (1997) *The Hungry Spirit*, Hutchinson, UK.
For many people, Charles Handy is the only genuine, internationally recognized management guru that these shores have produced. Those of us who have heard his contributions to the "Thought for the Day" slot on Radio 4's *Today* programme know him to be a decent, socially concerned man. Attacking Handy is a bit like speaking ill of a favorite uncle or, as Nick Cohen put it when reviewing this book in the *New Statesman*, "the critical equivalent of pushing Michael Palin into an acid bath."

*The Hungry Spirit* sees Handy drawing together his business and spiritual interests as he looks at how the rawer aspects of capitalism can co-exist with the search for an inner meaning to life. It is this combination that seems to have generated an unenthusiastic response from reviewers.

"Many of his ideas are worthy of support," wrote Peter Marsh in the *Financial Times* before concluding that the book was "a string of unsubstantiated, loosely connected anecdotes and ideas." Cohen's review, while acknowledging the author's benevolence, claims that "Handy has managed to climb the twin peaks of modern triteness ... first a consultant spouting management speak and then a radio preacher oozing platitudes."

Not all reviews were critical. *People Management* described *The Hungry Spirit* as "an important book" with "something in it for everyone" that "will make you think more deeply both about work and life."

In the final analysis, different readers will form different conclusions about *The Hungry Spirit*. Those who share Handy's quest for meaning in work and life will find much to applaud; more pragmatic readers in search of new business ideas will feel partially stimulated but ultimately short-changed.

Handy, Charles (1996) *The Search for Meaning*, Lemos & Crane, UK.

Handy, Charles (1994) *The Empty Raincoat*, Hutchinson, UK.
Contains some useful expansion of Handy's ideas about federal organizations.

Handy, Charles (1994) *Understanding Organizations* (4th edn), Penguin, UK.

# PAUL HAWKEN, AMORY B. LOVINS & L. HUNTER LOVINS

## Natural Capitalism

## 1999

Y ou and I know that genuinely original and insightful books are hard to find. So a book that claims that it portrays opportunities that, if captured, will lead to no less than a transformation of commerce and all societal institutions deserves a closer look.

The authors put forward a new approach for reconciling ecological and economic priorities, one that not only protects the earth's environment but also improves profits and competitiveness. "Not possible" is our first, and quite natural, response because we have been taught that environmental and economic priorities are contradictory. We strive, therefore at reaching a state of "balance," recognizing the natural trade-offs that exist. The authors argue otherwise, that the best solutions are based on design integration at all levels of economic activity. This principle recognizes not only human, financial and manufactured capital but also natural capital; the resources, living systems and ecosystem services of our world. This they call this approach "natural capitalism."

The book outlines four central strategies of natural capitalism, which are interrelated and interdependent. All four offer numerous benefits and opportunities in markets, finance, materials, distribution and employment:

1  *Radical resource productivity.* This is the cornerstone of natural capitalism. Fundamental changes in both production design and technology offer us the opportunity to develop ways to make natural resources – energy, minerals, water, forests – stretch 5, 10, even 100 times further than they do today.
2  *A shift to biologically inspired production models.* Bio-mimicry seeks not only to reduce waste but to eliminate the very concept of waste. In closed-loop production systems, modeled on nature's designs,

every output is returned harmlessly to the ecosystem as a nutrient, like compost, or becomes an input for manufacturing another product.

3  *A move to a solutions-based business model.* The business model of traditional manufacturing rests on the sale of goods. In the new model, value is instead delivered as a flow of services, which reduces consumption but improves consumer choice (for example, access to the entire music catalogues of music companies by subscription rather than purchasing individual CDs).

4  *Reinvesting in natural capital.* Sustaining, restoring and expanding natural stocks of capital to work towards reversing world-wide planetary destruction.

Accustomed as we are to so many business books promising us the moon, it is only natural that we have become somewhat cynical and jaded. *Natural Capitalism* is different. This book delivers.

### Reality check

"At its simplest, increasing resource productivity means obtaining the same amount of utility or work from a product or process while using less material or energy. In manufacturing, transportation, forestry, construction, energy, and other industrial sectors, mounting empirical evidence suggests that radical improvements in resource productivity are both practical and cost-effective, even in the most modern industries. Companies and designers are developing ways to make natural resources – energy, metals, waters and forests – work five, ten, even one hundred times harder than they do today. These efficiencies transcend the marginal gains in performance that industry constantly seeks as part of its evolution. Instead, revolutionary leaps in design and technology will alter industry itself."

Taken from *Natural Capitalism*

## The authors

Paul Hawken is an environmentalist, educator and best-selling author. He has served on the board of several organizations, including Conservation International, Friends of the Earth, and the National Audubon Society. He received the 1999 Green Cross Millennium Award for International Environmental Leadership.

Amory B. Lovins and L. Hunter Lovins are co-Chief Executive Officers of the Rocky Mountain Institute in Colorado, which they founded in 1982.

Consultants to several companies worldwide, they are co-authors (with Ernst von Weizsäcker) of the best-selling *Factor Four: Doubling Wealth, Halving Resource Use*.

Ernst von Weizsäcker (co-author of *Factor Four*) is President of the Wuppertal Institute for Climate, Environment and Energy in the North-Rhine/Westphalian Science Centre, Germany. He was previously Professor of Biology at Essen University. In 1996, he was the first recipient of the Duke of Edinburgh Gold Medal of WWF International.

## Sources and further reading

Hawken, Paul, Lovins, Amory B., and Lovins, L. Hunter (1999), *Natural Capitalism: the Next Industrial Revolution*, Earthscan Publications Ltd, UK.

von Weizsäcker, Ernst, Amory B., and Lovins, L. Hunter (1997), *Factor Four: Doubling Wealth, Halving Resource Use*, Earthscan Publications Ltd, UK.

First a definition of Factor Four: "Factor Four, in a nutshell, means that resource productivity can and should grow fourfold. The amount of wealth extracted from one unit of natural resources can quadruple. Thus we can live twice as well yet use half as much"

The practical promise held out in this book is huge, although it is up to businesses and governments, as well as each of us individually, to take it. Although not the easiest of reads, *Factor Four* does seem to be getting into the hands of political and social agenda-setters. It may prove to be a highly influential book over the coming decade, and certainly its underlying philosophy ought to appeal to the heads and pockets of the business community. Definitely a book to know about.

The publishers of both books have a useful Website which can be found at www.earthscan.co.uk

# MICHAEL DE KARE-SILVER

## E-Shock 2000 (2nd edition)

### 2000

 hen *E-Shock* first came out in 1998, some thought it a landmark book. It analyzed the impact of the electronic shopping revolution on retailers and manufacturers and the strategic for the future. *E-Shock 2000* has been revised and updated to take account of developments such as digital television, and to include interviews with some of the leading players in electronic shopping to have emerged over the past couple of years.

At the heart of the book are 12 major research findings and insights, all of which are examined in detail. De Kare-Silver's key findings are as follows:

1  The revolution in electronic shopping *is* going to happen: "All the evidence points to an unstoppable momentum, an inexorable force that will drive electronic commerce forward and reach out to make it so pervasive and accessible that it can't fail to impact shopping habits."

2  It's going to have a major impact on the shopping and retailing scene: "It's not going to be just another distribution channel or an experience confined to 35-year-old male computer nerds."

3  Already c. 15–20% of consumers say they'd prefer to shop electronically rather than visiting the shops: "Consumer research shows significant numbers of people instinctively appreciate the benefits of shopping electronically ... The underlying convenience is just too tempting to ignore."

4  It only takes a drop of c. 15% in store traffic to make many stores unprofitable: "Retail margins are often wafer thin ... retailers are very vulnerable to small shifts and reductions in the number of people who visit and shop at the store."

5 This revolution will achieve critical mass by as early as 2005: "Since the initial hype, more measured assessment has taken place. Most now agree that it is in the next decade that the real growth will come."

6 As store visits reduce, some shops are in danger of dying out; midsized high streets and malls are the most vulnerable: "Small high streets and shopping areas just won't be able to meet consumers' widening needs and expectations."

7 From supermarkets to banks, nearly all retailers will be affected: "The electronic shopping phenomenon....cuts across all retail consumer sectors with financial services one of the most vulnerable areas."

8 Not all is lost! Retailers can survive and succeed but need to decide which of ten identified strategic options they are going to pursue: "They range from a relatively low-key response through to aggressive investment in the new medium."

9 Manufacturers can seize the opportunity to decide whether to establish their own direct consumer distribution and bypass existing retail chains: "Electronic shopping presents manufacturers with an opportunity to fight back and re-establish their links with their end user."

10 The electronic environment will demand new marketing skills: "Guiding consumers to the specific Website will be a new challenge and making it easy once they get there the most critical point of leverage."

11 Future success urgently requires the development of a clear long-term strategy ...: "Immersion in the market place, understanding customers' needs and wants in a comprehensive way, identifying the various options and evaluating which will have the best leverage – these are all critical steps any player in the retail scene must now go through."

12 Rigorous implementation and communication: "For some companies, this may result in significant upheaval and new investment in systems and skills. But given the way electronic commerce is moving and the speed of its development there may be no choice."

Without the data and analysis that underpin these conclusions, de Kare-Silver's findings might appear a little glib and not terribly original. His findings do derive from solid looking research, and it should be remembered that his intention is to provide a practical guide to companies that are wondering whether and how to enter the virtual selling market place.

To help them make that decision, de Kare-Silver offers readers the ES Test – ES not surprisingly standing for electronic shopping. The test, which is set out in the book covers three elements:

1   *Product characteristics*, i.e. how the product appeals to the senses. Does it need to be tried or touched before buying? Products that appeal in the realms of sight and sound are most naturally suited to electronic shopping.
2   *Familiarity and confidence*, i.e. the extent to which the consumer recognizes and trusts the product, has used it before, and would be happy to repurchase.
3   *Consumer attributes*, i.e. how the consumer feels about the act of shopping. Would the consumer prefer to carry on physically visiting a shop rather than purchase electronically? Alternatively, is the consumer predisposed to shop electronically for whatever reason?

If the ES Test shows that a retailer's products or services have some potential to be purchased electronically, the retailer next needs to consider respond their options. In working with companies in this area, de Kare-Silver has identified ten alternative strategies or response options. They cover a range of initiatives from taking just a few small steps, through to the most radical involving a full switch of the business away from real estate to virtual shopping. The ten strategic options are:

1   *Information only.* Establishing a minimal presence, as much to respond to consumer enquiries as to protect turf against competitors.
2   *Export.* Ring-fencing existing domestic retail outlets but using ES to gain access to new markets and customers.
3   *Subsume into existing business.* Like 1 and 2, this does not seek to change existing operations; rather ES interest is integrated within the existing business.
4   *Treat as another channel.* With this option, ES is simply an alternative means to reach a target group of (probably existing) customers.
5   *Set up as separate business:* an important evolution from the previous step, this involves recognizing that it is a fundamentally different business requiring different skills and competencies to make it work.
6   *Pursue on all fronts.* Aggressively pursuing every sales channel that is available.
7   *Mixed system.* This approach could be called "Flagship stores + On-line delivery." It involves retaining a physical retail shopping

---

**Zeitbite**

A new generation is growing up digital. By the year 2000 there will be more than 88 million people in US and Canada between the ages of 2 and 22. They are the kids who are leading the charge using the new media that's centered around the Internet. This Net Generation is developing and imposing its culture on us thereby reshaping how society and individuals interact.

Don Tapscott, author of *Growing up Digital*, quoted in *E-Shock 2000*

---

presence of equal strategic importance to the ES channel. Examples include Tower Records, DKNY, and Disney

8 *Switch fully.* Taking the path of gradually but inexorably shifting away from physical retail sites to become a dedicated electronic trader. Examples include the British Airways physical travel shops and the AA, who closed all of its high street shops claiming that "people now prefer to do business over the telephone or Website."

9 *"Best of both."* This option assumes that most if not all existing stores can be retained alongside a developed electronic presence.

10 *Revitalize and buck the trend.* This option makes absolutely no concession to the forces of electronic retailing. Rather it takes a determinedly defensive stance towards the existing physical operation but looks to revitalize it so that consumers will want to continue to shop like they always did.

De Kare-Silver then goes on to offer advice on how to best implement the chosen strategy.

For those who find many e-shopping texts too highfalutin for their liking and who are looking for good, solid advice to help them think through the issues in a logical, step-by-step manner, *E-Shock 2000* takes a determinedly practical and pragmatic approach to what is fast becoming the most crucial strategic decision facing many retailers.

## The author

Michael de Kare-Silver advises companies on e-business development. He is a founding partner of the Kalchas Group, now part of Computer Sciences Corporation. A qualified commercial lawyer by training, he has also had spells working for McKinsey and Procter & Gamble. He is also the author of Strategy in Crisis (Macmillan Business, 1997).

## Sources and further reading

de Kare-Silver, Michael (2000) *E-Shock 2000*, Macmillan Business, UK.

# KEVIN KELLY

# New Rules for the New Economy

## 1998

I f the new economy needed to elect a founding father, Kevin Kelly
would be on most people's list of nominations. As the first editor of
*Wired* magazine in the early 1990s, Kelly quickly built a reputation
as one of the new economy's creators and biographers.

In *New Rules for the New Economy*, Kelly sets out to identify the
underlying principles that govern how the wired world operates. His
starting point is that ideas and assumptions about the nature of work
and the operating patterns of organizations that stem from the Age of
the Machine simply don't make sense in the revolutionary Age of the
Network. Success, maintains Kelly, flows primarily from understanding
networks – how they behave and the rules that govern them.

At the heart of the network revolution is communication. Kelly writes:

> "Communication is the foundation of society, of our culture,
> of our humanity, of our own individual identity, and of all
> economic systems. This is why networks are such a big deal.
> Communication is so close to culture and society itself that
> the effects of technologizing it are beyond the scale of a mere
> industrial-sector cycle. Communication, and its ally computers,
> is a special case in economic history. Not because it happens
> to be the fashionable leading business sector of our day, but
> because its cultural, technological, and conceptual impacts
> reverberate at the root of our lives."

*New Rules for the New Economy* takes the form of ten "rules," each given a
chapter in the book. Kelly formulated these guiding principles by asking
some fundamental questions: How do our tools shape our destiny? What

kind of economy is our new technology suggesting? What became clear to him was, he writes, that "Steel ingots and rivers of oil, smokestacks and factory lines, and even tiny seeds and cud-chewing cows are all becoming enmeshed in the world of smart chips and fast bandwidth, and sooner or later they will begin to fully obey the new rules."

The ten rules themselves are a pithy guide to business survival in the Internet age. But don't let the brevity of the book fool you – there is no evidence that Kelly has skimped on his thinking. In fact, one of his real talents is an ability to absorb and synthesize large amounts of information (his first book, *Out of Control*, came with a 300-title annotated bibliography at the back).

A definition of genius is the ability to look at the same world as everybody else and draw different conclusions. It's an ability that Kelly clearly has in abundance. Beyond that, as this lucid and awe-inspiring book shows, he is equally capable of reporting back what he sees. File under "New Economy Classic."

## Kevin Kelly's ten new rules for the new economy

1  *Embrace the swarm.* As power flows away from the center, the competitive advantage belongs to those who learn how to embrace decentralized points of control.

2  *Increasing returns.* As the number of connections between people and things add up, the consequences of those connections multiply out even faster, so that initial successes aren't self-limiting, but self-feeding.

3  *Plentitude, not scarcity.* As manufacturing techniques perfect the art of making copies plentiful, value is carried by abundance, rather than scarcity, inverting traditional business propositions.

4  *Follow the free.* As resource scarcity gives way to abundance, generosity begets wealth. Following the free rehearses the inevitable fall of prices, and takes advantage of the only true scarcity: human attention.

5  *Feed the web first.* As networks entangle all commerce, a firm's primary focus shifts from maximizing the firm's value to maximizing the network's value. Unless the net survives, the firm perishes.

6  *Let go at the top.* As innovation accelerates, abandoning the highly successful in order to escape from its eventual obsolescence becomes the most difficult and yet most essential task.

7 *From places to spaces.* As physical proximity (place) is replaced by multiple interactions with anything, anytime, anywhere (space), the opportunities for intermediaries, middlemen, and mid-size niches expand greatly.

8 *No harmony, all flux.* As turbulence and instability become the norm in business, the most effective survival stance is a constant but highly selective disruption that we call innovation.

9 *Relationship tech.* As the soft trumps the hard, the most powerful technologies are those that enhance, amplify, extend, augment, distil, recall, expand, and develop soft relationships of all types.

10 *Opportunities before efficiencies.* As fortunes are made by training machines to be ever more efficient, there is yet far greater wealth to be had by unleashing the inefficient discovery and creation of new opportunities.

## The author

Born in Pennsylvania and brought up in New Jersey, Kevin Kelly dropped out of college to spend 8 years trekking around India, Nepal, and the Far and Middle East. On his return the US, Kelly began to discover the on-line world, and through this he developed contacts that led to him being getting a job as Editor of *Whole Earth Review*, before going on to became Founding Editor at *Wired*. He left the role when the magazine was sold but remains an Editor-at-Large. He is reported to be working on a project to list all the 30 million or so species of life on earth.

## Sources and further reading

Kelly, Kevin (1998) *New Rules for the New Economy: 10 Ways the Network Economy is Changing Everything*, Fourth Estate, UK.

Kelly, Kevin (1994) *Out of Control: the New Biology of Machines*, Addison Wesley Inc, USA.
*Out of Control* is a sprawling, provocative, and massive (at over 600 pages) exploration of the organic nature of human-made systems. It's crammed with original insights all clustered around Kelly's view that our technological future is headed toward a neo-biological civilization. There are those who would argue that this is Kelly's true masterpiece.

Kelly has a Website at www.well.com/user/kk/ and the full text of *Out of Control* can be found at www.well.com/user/kk/OutOfControl/

Davidson, Andrew, "The net prophet," *Financial Times*, 3 June 2000. Highly readable and informative article about Kelly.

# CHARLES LEADBEATER

## *Living on Thin Air*

### 1999

**W**hat do you make to earn your living? Do you make anything tangible that can be weighed, measured or touched? For most people, says Charles Leadbeater, the answer to the second question is no, with more and more of us making our living from thin air – from our ideas and our know-how. "Knowledge," states Leadbeater, "is our most precious resource: we should organise society to maximise its creation and use. Our aim should be to harness the power of markets and community to the more fundamental goals of creating and spreading knowledge."

In *Living on Thin Air*, Leadbeater explores the societal implications of a knowledge-driven economy, coming as it does at a time of increasing economic and job insecurity. He argues that society will need to be organized around the creation of knowledge capital and social capital, rather than simply being dominated by the power of financial capital: "When financial, social and knowledge capital work in harmony, through institutions designed to reconcile their competing demand, society will be strong. When these forces are at war, society will malfunction. A society devoted to financial capitalism will be unbalanced and soulless. A society devoted to social solidarity will stagnate, lacking the dynamism of radical new ideas and the discipline of the competitive market. A society devoted solely to knowledge creation would be intelligent but poor, even if it did realize the value of its know-how to the full. When these three forces of the new economy work together, they can be hugely dynamic. Too often they seem in danger either of spinning out of control or of being trapped by a society unable to stomach the institutional reforms needed to move forward. That is where we are, trapped between the gridlock of the old and the chaos of the new."

To support this call to action, Leadbeater draws on research in California, Japan, Germany and the Far East to show how his provocative manifesto might be achieved. He puts over his ideas in a highly informative and accessible way and argues his case well, although some readers may feel that his take on the future is a tad more optimistic than the facts seem to justify.

## The author

Charles Leadbeater is an independent writer, a research associate for UK think-tank Demos, and a new economy consultant to leading companies. Previously, he was Industrial Editor and Tokyo Bureau Chief at the *Financial Times* before moving on the *Independent*, where he devised *Bridget Jones's Diary* with Helen Fielding. In 1998, he helped Peter Mandelson, then Secretary of State at the Department of Trade and Industry, to develop a White Paper entitled "Building the Knowledge Driven Economy."

## Sources and further reading

Leadbeater, Charles (1999) *Living on Thin Air*, Viking, UK.

Leadbeater, Charles, & Oakley, Kate (1999) *The Independents: Britain's New Cultural Entrepreneurs*, Demos, UK.
In this latest pamphlet from independent think tank Demos, Leadbeater and co-author Kate Oakley explore how a growing share of some of the fastest growing sectors of the British economy is accounted for by a new and independent breed of cultural entrepreneurs. Across Britain, thousands of young people are working from bedrooms, workshops and run-down offices, hoping that they will come up with the next Hotmail or Netscape, the next Lara Croft, or the next Wallace and Gromit. This group – labeled *The Independents* by the authors – are typically in their twenties and thirties and have emerged from a convergence of three forces:

1   *Technology.* This is the first generation that grew up with computers and that understand how to reap the benefits of modern computing power and communications. In earlier decades, increased computer power primarily benefited large organizations. The Independents feel enabled, not threatened, by new technology.

2    *Values.* The Independents are typically anti-establishment, anti-traditionalist and highly individualistic. Those values pre-dispose them to pursue self-employment and entrepreneurship in a spirit of self-exploration and self-fulfillment.
3    *Economics.* They have entered the workforce from the late 1980s onwards, during which time self employment and entrepreneurship have become very attractive alternatives to careers in large, impersonal, frequently downsizing organizations.

For some compelling examples of 21st-century working life conveyed concisely, *The Independents* is well worth a read.

For further information or to purchase a copy, e-mail: mail@demos.co.uk

# RICK LEVINE, CHRISTOPHER LOCKE, DOC SEARLS & DAVID WEINBERGER

## *The Cluetrain Manifesto*

## 2000

his is what *The Cluetrain Manifesto* isn't. It's not a feel-good book, not a how-to book, and it's not boring. So says Tom Petzinger, author of *The New Pioneers*, writing in the book's foreword.

So what is it?

- It's a manifesto for the Internet generation.
- It's a virus.
- It's a series of charges against the corporate sector.
- It's a declaration of human rights for inhabitants of the business and technology world.
- It's riddled with Americanisms.
- It's a book written as a sequel to a Website.
- It's loud, frequently over the top, but equally often challenging.
- It's a book with a stellar cast of admirers from the business world (Esther Dyson, Thomas Stewart, to name two).
- It is the only business book that begins with the greeting "People of Earth."
- It's a set of 95 theses.
- It's laugh-out-loud funny in places.

(Given that irony is both the most common mode of communication used on the Internet and indeed in *The Cluetrain Manifesto*, it was tempting to carry on with the bullet-points until there were 95 – matching the number of theses or principles that comprise the manifesto. But don't worry, a saner writing style will prevail.)

The story of *The Cluetrain Manifesto* goes like this: it began in the early part of 1999 when the book's authors – four respected insiders from the technology sector – decided to use a Website as a forum for articulating what they described as "a set of principles we believe will determine the future experience of both individuals and organizations online." The principles, a mixture of declarations that business is fundamentally a human enterprise, and devastating swipes at a business establishment seemingly intent on viewing the Internet as a marketplace to colonize rather than a community to join.

They compiled their manifesto, published it to a Website, and invited visitors to the site to sign up to it. Word about the site spread virally through corporate America, and the site rapidly attained a cult status. Scrolling through the signatories reveals names from companies like IBM, PriceWaterhouseCoopers and Adobe Systems (in fact a good chunk of the *Fortune* 500 is represented).

The book, published in 2000, gave the authors the opportunity to expand and augment the contents of the manifesto. They do this through seven chapters filled with their stories and observations about how business gets done in and how the Internet will change it all. Like the Manifesto itself, the book is a great read but stylistically and content-wise it's more of the same. The authors offer no real analysis, no models, no real frameworks. The book is self-referential (no bibliography, no index), making no attempt to draw on other business thinkers to provide some theoretical underpinning. Some readers will welcome this absolute self-confidence in their own point of view. Others may feel that this makes the conversation a little one-sided and shallow.

### *The Cluetrain Manifesto*: a selection of the 95 theses

- Markets are conversations.
- Markets consist of human beings, not demographic sectors.
- Conversations among human beings *sound* human. They are conducted in a human voice.
- The Internet is enabling conversations among human beings that were simply not possible in the era of mass media.
- In just a few more years, the current homogenized "voice" of business – the sound of mission statements and brochures – will seem as contrived and artificial as the language of the 18th-century French court.
- Companies that assume online markets are the same markets that used to watch their ads on television are kidding themselves.
- Companies can now communicate with their markets directly. If they blow it, it could be their last chance.

- Companies attempting to "position" themselves need to *take* a position. Optimally, it should relate to something their market actually cares about.
- Public relations does not relate to the public. Companies are deeply afraid of their markets.
- Brand loyalty is the corporate version of going steady, but the breakup is inevitable – and coming fast. Because they are networked, smart markets are able to renegotiate relationships with blinding speed.
- Networked markets can change suppliers overnight. Networked knowledge workers can change employers over lunch. Your own "downsizing initiatives" taught us to ask the question: "Loyalty? What's that?"
- Today, the organization chart is hyperlinked, not hierarchical. Respect for hands-on knowledge wins over respect for abstract authority.
- We want access to your corporate information, to your plans and strategies, your best thinking, your genuine knowledge. We will not settle for the four-color brochure, for Websites chock-a-block with eye candy but lacking any substance.
- Maybe you're impressing your investors. Maybe you're impressing Wall Street. You're not impressing us.
- We like this new marketplace much better. In fact, we are creating it.
- Have you noticed that, in itself, money is kind of one-dimensional and boring? What else can we talk about?
- We want you to take 50 million of us as seriously as you take one reporter from the *Wall Street Journal*.
- Our allegiance is to ourselves – our friends, our new allies and acquaintances, even our sparring partners. Companies that have no part in this world, also have no future.
- We are waking up and linking to each other. We are watching. But we are not waiting.

## The authors

Rick Levin is co-founder and CTO of Mancal Inc. Prior to this, he was Web Architect for Sun Microsystems' Java Software Group. He is also author of *The Sun Guide to Web Style*.

Christopher Locke publishes *Entropy Gradient Reversals* from Boulder, Colorado. He has written extensively for publications such as *Forbes*,

*Byte, Internet World* and the *Industry Standard.* In the past, he has worked for a number of companies, including Fujitsu, Ricoh, MCI, and IBM

Doc Searls is the senior editor for *Linux Journal.* He is a marketing veteran who co-founded Hodskins Simone and Searls, one of Silicon Valley's leading advertising agencies for many years.

David Weinberger is the publisher of *JOHO* (*Journal of the Hyper-linked Organization*). He has written for a wide variety of publications, notably *Wired* and *The New York Times.*

## Sources and further reading

Levine, Rick, Locke, Christopher, Searls, Doc and Weinberger, David (2000) *The Cluetrain Manifesto: the End of Business as Usual,* Perseus Publishing, USA.
The Website address is www.cluetrain.com

# MICHAEL LEWIS
## *The New New Thing*
### 1999

P art-biography, part-adventure story, part-business book, *The New New Thing* is a vivid portrayal of billionaire Jim Clark, one of the Silicon Valley super-rich. Clark is the serial entrepreneur who founded Netscape and Silicon Graphics and who, at the time that the book was being written, was aiming to turn the $1 trillion dollar US healthcare industry on its head with his new project, Healtheon.

When Jim Clark decided to take Netscape public just 18 months after forming the company in 1994, despite it having no profits and no revenue to speak of, he rewrote the laws of capitalism by showing that massive growth was more critical than the need to show profits. The Netscape flotation, on August 9, 1995, remains perhaps the most famous share offering in the American stock market's history. It was a huge success with the company's stock doubling in value within less than 24 hours. It also set the scene for a series of high-profile flotations by, amongst others, eBay, priceline.com and MarketWatch.

Given that Clark is a Silicon Valley legend, and that Michael Lewis was supposed to be writing about how Clark was going to create in Healtheon a vehicle for bringing the vast majority of the healthcare industry's transactions online, *The New New Thing* is disappointingly light on business insights. Although Clark's success as an entrepreneurial businessman goes without saying, any budding high-tech entrepreneur looking for lessons from how he managed to make his fortune will be disappointed. Perhaps Lewis should have conducted a series of probing question and answer interviews with Clark and those that know him or had dealings with him. From the questions he does ask, it's clear that Lewis has a sharp mind, but he is no Jeremy Paxman when it comes to interview technique

That said, we do get the occasional glimpse into the inner workings of Silicon Valley. For example, Lewis gives a fascinating insight into the practices of Silicon Valley venture capitalists – and a more venal, vicious bunch you're unlikely ever to meet. Clark's strategy for dealing with them – sell the dream, not the business plan, and you're in – is all very well and works for him. But in terms of business lessons for the general reader, you can take it that no VC is going to treat you the way Clark is treated – unless you too are worth a few billion.

So what does *The New New Thing* tell us about the new economy? That Clark is its Citizen Kane? That the aura and mystique of a larger-than-life character like Clark plays a bigger part in selling a business idea than a convincing business plan? That Silicon Valley, the engine-room of the new economy, has a surreal sense of business logic?

The curiosity is that of the three enterprises Clark is most closely associated with, Silicon Graphics is struggling to survive, Netscape has been sold to online giant AOL, and Healtheon still making a loss.

### (Un)reality check: more than enough is not enough

"This was news. I pointed out that he'd never before mentioned this ambition. 'I just want to have more money than Larry Ellison,' he said again. 'I don't know why. But once I have more money than Larry Ellison, I'll be satisfied.' Larry Ellison, the CEO of Oracle, the biggest software company in the Valley, was worth about nine billion dollars; Clark was worth a bit more than three billion. On the other hand, Ellison's wealth was completely tied up in Oracle Stock, which had mostly missed out on the boom. At the rate Clark's wealth was grow-ing, he'd pass Ellison within six months. I pointed this out and asked the obvious question: 'What happens after you have more than Larry Ellison? Would you want to have more money than, say, Bill Gates?' 'Oh, no,' Clark said, waving my question to the side of the room where the ridiculous ideas gather to commiserate with each other. 'That'll never happen.' A few minutes later, after the conversation had turned to other matters, he came clean. 'You know,' he said, 'just for one moment, I would kind of like to have the most. Just for one tiny moment.'

"It was one of those tiny moments when it was good to have a record of our conversations. Just a few months before, when he was worth a mere $600 million, Clark had said, 'I just want to have a billion dollars, after taxes. Then I'll be satisfied.'"

Taken from *The New New Thing*

**Zeitbite**

The moment of conception was, to Clark's way of thinking, the critical moment of any new enterprise. At that moment it was important not merely to hire the people bent on changing the world but to avoid hiring the people bent only on changing jobs.

"There are all sorts of guys who will show up because they can't think of anything else to do," he said. "Those are exactly the people you don't want. I have a strategy for dealing with these people. When they come by to apply for a job I tell them, "We're all confused here. We don't know what we're going to do yet." But when you find someone you want, I tell them, "Here's exactly what we're going to do and it is going to be *huge* and you are going to get very, very rich."

## The author

Michael Lewis is a visiting fellow at the University of California at Berkeley.

He is the author of *Liar's Poker*, a searing and often very funny book about life on the trading floor at a Wall Street investment bank

## Sources and further reading

Lewis, Michael (1999) *The New New Thing: How Some Man You've Never Heard Of Just Changed Your Life*, W W Norton, USA.

Collins, James C. (March 2000) "Built to flip," *Fast Company*, Issue 32.

Quittner, Joshua and Slatalla, Michelle (1998) *Speeding the Net*, Atlantic Monthly Press, USA.
Worth reading for a more detailed insight into Jim Clark in the Netscape days. Written by the technology editors from *Time* magazine and the *New York Times*, respectively.

# GERRY McGOVERN
## *The Caring Economy*
### 1999

G erry McGovern makes clear his perspective on the new economy very early on in his book, writing as follows:

> "*The Caring Economy* is not a book about computers or the Internet. It's not about information technology and e-commerce. It's not about more bandwidth and faster processors. It's not about digital television or video-on-demand. It's not about nerds and hackers. It's not a book about cost savings and downsizing and automating people out of the picture ... Rather, it is a book about people (business people and consumer people) and how we all interact on the Internet. It's a book that explores the relationship between people and the tools they make and use. It's about how people are impacted by, and impact on, new technologies and issues. It's a book that seeks to establish some philosophical foundations and basic principles for living in the digital age. It's a book about how we all need new attitudes, new rules and new business principles for success in a digital age economy and society."

McGovern believes that "community and commerce are inherently intertwined; that you can't have one without the other." For him, what drives the Internet is not technology, it's the human touch. This aspect is amplified in what he calls *The Caring Economy*'s set of "Internet Business Principles," 10 points that are intended to help guide the reader's thinking and actions in the new economy.

However, *The Caring Economy* is more than a touchy-feely take on the information economy. McGovern may wear his heart and values on his sleeve, but behind the compassion is a keen, insightful and analyti-

---

**Zeitbite**

Perhaps *the* fundamental principle for success in the digital age is to *think network*."

Gerry McGovern, *The Caring Economy*

---

cal intelligence that he applies to a range of issues: the history of the Internet; the nature of cyberspace, truths and myths of the information society, globalization, the strength and limitations of computers – all these themes, and more besides, are covered. And, in case that list gives the impression that McGovern is a "big themes" man, he also offers practical and implementable advice on making best use of the Internet, including a particularly good section on building brands online.

But in the final analysis, it is McGovern's demonstrable humanity that distinguishes this book. A colleague who cast an eye over the list of authors featured in *Writing the New Economy* told me that, while he admired the industry experience and subject matter expertise of those represented, "there aren't that many people there that you would want to sit down and share a pint with in a pub." My round, Gerry.

### Gerry McGovern's ten Internet business principles

1   Care. Care about your customers. Care about your staff. Care about all those connected with you. Put people first because people are where you will find your unique competitive advantage.
2   Empower all those connected with you and where appropriate create communities which allow you to organize around the consumer, rather than around a product or service offering.
3   Champion and focus on old people, women and children who are three key engines in *The Caring Economy*. Also, focus on niches and communities of interest, delivering unique products and services. In the digital age, it will pay to specialize.
4   Focus on the value you deliver, not just the costs you save. Remember, the Internet is not cheap to develop for, requiring quality brands, quality people and substantial ongoing investment.

5   Let your information flow by focusing on the three properties of information: content, structure and publication. Use information quickly and gain value from the momentum it creates.

6   Keep the communication of your information as simple as possible. Cut through the hype and don't fall into the trap of being complicated in a complex age.

7   Think digital and study the lessons that are being learnt in software development. Learn from the Internet too. Remember, the best way to succeed on the Internet is to imitate how the Internet itself became a success and this means thinking network.

8   Learn to play, challenge the unchallengeable, think the unthinkable and encourage the heretic. Evangelize and bring other people with you. Embrace change and flow with the age.

9   Protect and build your brand and good name. Trust is not easy to establish on the Internet and those who gain the consumer's trust will reap the long-term rewards.

10  Have a long-term vision of where you want to go. Don't forget the information-poor consumer. Remember that we are citizens of an increasingly connected world. For the long-term stability and prosperity of our world, we cannot continue to ignore the injustice, poverty and famine that so many of our fellow citizens must daily endure.

Taken from *The Caring Economy*

## The author

Gerry McGovern is Chief Executive Officer of Nua, a company that specializes in Internet-driven knowledge management solutions. Born in Ireland in 1962, he gained a Bachelor of Science in Management from Trinity College, Dublin. After leaving college in 1984, he worked in business for a while before leaving to write fiction and travel. In 1994, he wrote a report for the Irish government called "Ireland: the Digital Age, the Internet." In the following year, he and two colleagues founded Nua. He can be contacted at gerry@nua.ie

## Sources and further reading

McGovern, Gerry (1999) *The Caring Economy*, Blackhall Publishing, Ireland.
The book has a companion Website at www.thecaringeconomy.com/

McGovern writes a free, weekly e-mail newsletter called *New Thinking*, which aims to contribute towards the development of a digital age business philosophy. To subscribe, send an e-mail to: newthinking-request@nua.ie with the word "subscribe" in the body of the message

The address for Nua, the Internet development company co-founded by McGovern, is www.nua.com

# REGIS McKENNA

## *Real Time*

### 1997

T here's a Marx Brothers' film – *A Night in Casablanca* – where Groucho is hired to run a hotel whose previous managers have all wound up being murdered. Shortly after arriving, he makes an announcement to staff, which, from memory, goes along the lines of: "There are going to have to be some changes around here: from now on, if a guest asks for a three-minute egg, give them a two-minute egg; if they ask for a two-minute egg, give them a one-minute egg; and if they ask for a one-minute egg, give them the chicken and tell them to work it out for themselves."

Although in that case Groucho's motives were more profit- than customer-driven, most modern-day managers know that we are living in an age of ever more demanding customers. They want better quality, they want cheaper prices and, above all, they want it now. The bookshop owner who tells a customer that it will take two weeks to order in the book they want is seeing business go to Internet sites like Amazon. Until very recently, you had physically to go to a bank to get a balance on your account; now it's available on-line, more or less instantly.

Providing an immediate, customer-satisfying response to any request is a tough challenge for any business. But, says Regis McKenna, companies who wish to remain in the marketplace have only one choice in a world of instant gratification and infinite opportunity – they must become a real time business or perish.

How are companies to achieve this transformation? Having great technology will help to compress time, says McKenna, but just as critically companies must challenge conventional wisdom about how they operate. Traditional facets of company life – hierarchy, long-term planning methodologies – need to go, to be replaced by "real time managers" who focus on delivery and results, and who recognize that customized service is the new corporate mantra. Getting more specific, McKenna goes on to provide examples and ideas from companies that have gained a practical understanding of how time, technology and customer service are inter-related.

The book's contents are neatly summed up at regular intervals by a number of what McKenna calls "the real time message." To give a flavor, here are a few examples.

## On creating the real time company

"The task of implementing a real time corporation is difficult and complex, but it is an essential investment in your competitive future. The implementation of real time systems will have the effect of changing the working relationships within your organization as well as those with your partners and customers. The application of the technology will change your corporate culture. As these systems are adopted, new ideas for services and products, new ways of gaining customer loyalty, and new methods of team collaboration will take shape. Then information technology will indeed become a valued corporate asset."

## On technology and society

"The task of implementing a real time corporation is difficult and complex, but it is an essential investment in your competitive future. The implementation of real time systems will have the effect of changing the working relationships within your organization as well as those with your partners and customers. The application of the technology will change your corporate culture. As these systems are adopted, new ideas for services and products, new ways of gaining customer loyalty, and new methods of team collaboration will take shape. Then information technology will indeed become a valued corporate asset."

## On satisfying the never satisfied customer

"New consumers are never satisfied consumers. Managers hoping to serve them must work to eliminate time and space

## Zeitbite

Winning organizations will be run in the expectation of relentless shifts and readjustments in the marketplace, in customers' expectations, and in the behavior of competitors. Like Lewis Carroll's Queen, they will anticipate surprises six times a day before breakfast.

Regis McKenna

constraints on service. They must push the technological bandwidth with interactive dialogue systems – equipped with advanced software interfaces – in the interest of forging more intimate ties with these consumers. Managers must exploit every available means to obtain their end: building self-satisfaction capabilities into services and products and providing customers with access anytime, anywhere."

## On being prepared for anything

"Companies will learn about the technologies of real time in the only way they truly can – by adopting them and putting them to practical use. They will deploy them not to predict the future but to live virtually on top of changing patterns and trends affecting every sphere of their business environment, making rapid and continuous refinements in their way of doing business."

When *Real Time* was first published, it received excellent reviews in America, and a number of well-respected CEOs – including Fred Smith of Federal Express and HP's Lew Platt – sang its praises ("McKenna's insights will excite and shock you," said Platt). Although the messages of the book seem far less radical now than three years ago, McKenna's analysis remains just as valid, as does his emphasis on customized service and time-based competition. Companies that turn away from McKenna's prescription may well come in time to face the corporate significance of another of Groucho's lines – "I've had a wonderful evening, but this wasn't it."

## The author

Regis McKenna is Chairman of The McKenna Group, based in Palo Alto, California. He regularly lectures and conducts seminars on technology marketing and competitiveness. McKenna is the author of three other books – *The Regis Touch*, *Who's Afraid of Big Blue?* and *Relationship Marketing*.

## Sources and further reading

McKenna, Regis (1997) *Real Time: Preparing for the Age of the Never Satisfied Customer*, Harvard Business School Press, USA.
www.mckenna-group.com

# JOHN MICKLETHWAIT & ADRIAN WOOLDRIDGE

## A Future Perfect

## 2000

G lobalization has had a mixed press in recent times: on the one hand resented and denounced, most forcibly at the demonstrations during the World Trade Organization meeting in Seattle in November 1999; on the other hand seen as desirable and, in any case, inevitable.

John Micklethwait and Adrian Wooldridge, who both work at the *Economist*, make their stance clear from the outset of *A Future Perfect*. They write in their introduction:

> "This book has two aims. The first is to apply some order to the maelstrom of facts, images and opinions concerning globalization. In part that means unraveling some of the myths that have been built up about it: that is ushering in an age of global products; that it has killed inflation and changed the rules of economics; that big, local companies will crush their smaller rivals; and that geography means nothing in an age of rootless capitalism. Rather than treat globalization as one great co-ordinated movement – or, even more misleadingly, as an accomplished fact – we will argue that it should be seen as a series of waves, rather like the industrial revolution ... The second aim of this book is to make [an] intellectual case for globalization. For many economists – perhaps too many – that project is too easy to waste time over. Of course globalization makes sense: it leads to a more efficient use of resources; any student who understands the basic tenets of comparative advantage understands that. Though hard to dispute this argument seems inadequate for two reasons. First, it fails to confront the harsh questions concerning those people who lose

on account of globalization, not just economically but socially and culturally. And, second, it undersells globalization: the process has not to do only with economic efficiency; it has to do with freedom. Globalization offers the chance to fulfil (or at least come considerably closer to fulfilling) the goals that classical liberal philosophers first identified several centuries ago and that still underpin Western democracy."

Embracing these two aims, Micklethwait and Wooldridge take us on a global journey, ranging from the shanty towns of Sao Paulo to a London townhouse that has revolutionized the telecommunications industry, and from the borders of Russia to the sex industry in the San Fernando valley. In the course of this journey, they explore some of the central issues at the heart of the globalization debate. Can the nation-state survive the politics of interdependence? Should businesses go global and what are the secrets of business success in a global age? Are we creating a winner-take-all society? What should and what can be done about the losers from globalization? Will junk culture triumph in the future? Why is the UN so weak? And what will happen to your career?

*A Future Perfect* unveils a new meritocratic global ruling class which it dubs "the Cosmocrats": but it also addresses the losers – from car workers in the US to the environment in Bangkok. It also looks at the first version of globalization (1890–1913) and why it collapsed, before going on to explore what they call the three engines of globalization – technology, the capital markets, and management.

Micklethwait and Wooldridge make the vital point that the globalization debate is about more than economics. There is a fundamental issue about human freedom. They express their concern at "restrictions on where people can go, what they can buy, where they can invest, and what they can read, hear, or see. Globalization by its nature brings down these barriers, and it helps to hand the power to choose to the individual."

Given where they both work, it's not surprising that *A Future Perfect* reads like a good article in the *Economist* – incisive, intelligently argued, and extremely well written. They marshal their facts brilliantly and express their argument cogently. There are too many books and articles about globalization where the reader is little the wiser at the end. This book is a real exception and, for now at least, is the best and most balanced overview of the topic on the market.

## The authors

John Micklethwait is the London-based US Editor on the *Economist*. Adrian Wooldridge is Washington correspondent for the *Economist*. *A Future Perfect* marks their second collaboration. Their first was *The Witch Doctors*, an award-winning book on management gurus.

## Sources and further reading

Micklethwait, John and Wooldridge, Adrian (2000) *A Future Perfect: The Challenge and Hidden Promise of Globalization*, Heinemann, UK.
Micklethwait, John and Wooldridge, Adrian (1996) *The Witch Doctors*, Heinemann, UK.

### Reality Check: globalization, schmobalization?

"Globalisation has always primarily been a process of Westernisation,"

Gerald Segal, International Institute for Strategic Studies, www.isn.eethz.ch/iiss/

"America's biggest export is no longer the fruit of its fields or the output of its factories, but the mass produced products of its popular culture – movies and music, television programs, books and computer software. Entertainment around the globe is dominated by American-made products ... International sales of software and entertainment products totaled US\$60.2 billion in 1996, more than any other US industry ... Films produced in English account for between 60 and 65 per cent of the global box office, according to the Motion Picture Association of America; most of these ticket sales are generated by American-made films."

From an article entitled "The world welcomes America's cultural invasion," *International Herald Tribune*, www.iht.com

"As the world becomes more universal, it also becomes more tribal. As people yield economic sovereignty and become economically interdependent, holding on to what distinguishes you from others becomes very important."

John Naisbitt, from his book *Global Paradox*

"On a typical day in 1898, *The Times* of London led with its usual front page of advertisements; it then carried a page reviewing some recent novels; and then acres of coverage of the Balkan War. Altogether, the newspaper had nineteen columns of foreign news, eight columns of domestic news and three about salmon fishing. Exactly 50 years later, the front page still carried advertisements and the leaders commented on Italy, Canada, China and the crisis in Western civilisation (no change, then). By 1998, the advertisements on the front page had been replaced by articles. There were six of them and only one was foreign; it was about Leonardo DiCaprio's new girlfriend."

*Economist*, July 4, 1998

"I think that in many respects, globalisation is still superficial. Although there is a great deal of talk about it currently, the underlying truth is that the global economy is still limited. It seems to me that the real layer of globalisation is restricted to the capital markets. In most other areas, institutions remain intensely local ... Trade, for example, is still predominantly regional."

Francis Fukuyama, speaking at the Merrill Lynch Forum in 1998, www.ml.com/woml/forum/global.htm

# MARY MODAHL

## *Now or Never*

## 2000

I t is a conceit of each passing business generation to imagine that they have to contend with the toughest trading and working conditions ever known. Compared to now, we say, didn't our parents have it easy back in the sixties, the seventies, the eighties, and so on.

Doubtless, children of the current business generation will have legitimate reasons for feeling they merit the accolade, but even they might concede that, looking back, the first decade of the 21st century was a particularly turbulent period.

From her perch as Vice President of Research at Forrester Research Inc., a company at the forefront in providing research, analysis and advice on the business realities of new media and new technology, Mary Modahl is well placed to know what might lie ahead. Her view, explored in detail in *Now or Never*, is that the coming ten years will be a make-or-break period for many companies, well-established household names and business start-ups alike.

The growth in Internet commerce, she says, is spawning a set of trends that all companies will have to confront. Some examples:

- New pricing models undermine existing revenues with many Internet companies gambling that they can charge can lower prices and make up revenues on volume.
- Higher customer-service expectations. Internet businesses are open 24 hours a day, seven days a week, and so consumers can make purchasing choices at a time that suits them, having helped themselves to information about products before buying.
- New ways to distribute products. Internet companies build their businesses around home delivery – even in markets where home

delivery has never existed before. This has caught traditional companies, which focus on consumers' in-store experience, off guard.

- Unexpected market opportunities. Because the Internet connects people across very wide distances at extremely low cost, start-ups can dream up services that literally were never possible before.
- High rates of entry – even in very staid markets. Conservative industries such as newspaper classified advertising, which had not seen a significant entrant in decades, find themselves challenged by newcomers.

These trends set the stage for the battle for Internet consumers – a conflict, writes Modahl, "that will span more than ten years as companies adjust their strategies to take advantage of the Internet's ability to let consumers buy anytime, anywhere. On one side of this battle stand the established corporations – companies and brands that people have known since childhood. On the other, stand the 'dot.coms,' start-ups that believe they can offer consumers a better deal and become a household name in the process."

The battlefield is uneven, Modahl thinks: "Start-ups, with their Internet birthright, have the advantage. Being small, newer companies can move quickly, and their entire business revolves around a single focus. In addition, start-ups have had easy access to venture funding and more risk-tolerant investors than traditional companies. But most important, the dot.coms have nothing to lose if the old ways of doing business fade away." In contrast, she says, "Traditional companies have developed a core of well-understood business practices. Although this core is valuable, it also creates a gravity field, trapping the company by continually pulling it back toward the way it has always done business."

All, however, is not lost for the traditional companies. The Internet changes many business rules, but some fundamentals remain – knowing the customer, adding real value, differentiating from competitors, etc. The successful companies, dot.com or traditional, Modahl believes, will be those – old or new – that can understand Internet consumers, exploit Internet business models, and defy the gravity of the old ways of doing business.

The crucial first step to success in the Internet economy, she says, is understanding that the Internet consumer is an entirely new entity. Modahl claims that conventional demographic methods, which segment populations according to their age, social grouping, education etc., are poor predictors of online behavior. Instead, drawing on research conducted by Forrester, she puts forward a system called "technographics," which measures consumers' attitudes towards technology. One measure, for example, explores whether consumers feel positive or negative – Forrester found that 52% of the population is optimistic about technology and is "marching happily towards online shopping." Another crucial distinction is whether Internet consumers are motivated by career, family or entertainment needs. Not surprisingly, income level is also a significant factor.

Putting these elements together, Modahl and Forrester have come up with 10 types of Internet Consumer, including categories like the Fast Forwards (high-income optimists motivated by career needs), Traditionalists (high-income pessimists focused on nurturing their family and community relationships), Media Junkies (high-income pessimists focused on feeding their appetite for fun but who don't see technology as a way to meet their needs), and Sidelined Citizens. The book contains extensive analysis to help the reader understand the drivers of the various groupings and how to target them.

The Forrester system of "technographics" is the most interesting part of *Now or Never*, but Modahl is equally sound writing on Internet business models and offers convincing, research-based advice that enables the reader to select which approach might suit their business.

All in all, *Now or Never* provides some thoroughly convincing models, ideas and practical advice on how to excel in the Internet economy, and fully justifies Modahl as one of the premier and incisive analysts in the e-commerce field. And let's face it: those people working for companies that do succeed over the next few years will have something to tell their children about.

## Success in the Internet economy – the challenges

"Internet start-ups must grow at a breathtaking pace to support their investors' expectations. For these newly formed companies, there is no choice but to acquire customers and revenue as fast as possible – and most do so at the cost of ever widening losses. Traditional players must defend their customer base as they try to re-gear their company around the new business models. In most cases, this makeover requires cutting prices, improving service, and reducing costs faster than ever before. In short, the Internet makes consumer industries far more competitive and dynamic than they were in the past.

"As this day-to-day rivalry intensifies, it will become more important to step back and identify the sources of long-term value. Simply running like mad to sign up customers may be rewarded in the short run, particularly since the economies of scale in Internet businesses are so pronounced. Gaining market share, however, is not enough. Internet businesses are not natural monopolies, and there is no rule that states that once a company has acquired its customers, it can relax and go back to pricing above cost. Entry barriers remain low, and the key assets that Internet companies build – brand awareness and technological know-how – can be fumbled away in a single year."

Taken from *Now or Never*

## The author

Mary Modahl is Vice President of Research at Forrester Research Inc., a provider of primary research, market analysis, and strategic guidance in the area of electronic commerce. She is an influential and often-quoted industry figure whose work on the Internet economy embraces media, interactive software technologies and business trade. She lives in Concord, Massachusetts, with her husband and two children.

## Sources and further reading

Modahl, Mary (2000) *Now or Never: How Companies Must Change Today to Win the Battle for the Internet Customer*, HarperCollins, USA.

# GEOFFREY A. MOORE

# *Crossing the Chasm*

## 1991

C anadian songwriter Leonard Cohen tells a story of a time some years back when he was on a ferry travelling between Greek islands. While wandering around on deck, he heard somebody with a guitar giving a rendition of "Suzanne," one of his most popular songs, to a group of friends. Cohen says that was the moment when he knew that he no longer owned the song – it belonged to the world.

Geoffrey Moore might well feel the same about his most famous model – the Technology Adoption Life Cycle. First unveiled in *Crossing the Chasm*, the model describes five groups – Innovators, Early Adopters, Early Majority, Late Majority and Laggards – that are, in Moore's words, "distinguished from each other by their characteristic response to a discontinuous innovation based on a new technology." The model has been widely adopted and adapted, appearing in various guises. In her book *Now or Never*, for example, Mary Modahl of Forrest Researcher divides a company's consumer base into three categories – Early Adopters, Mainstream, and Laggards.

Like any model that has been widely used and popularized, sometimes the precision and intention of the original version gets overlooked. So it is worth reiterating Moore's model as it was intended. The first point to emphasize is that the model was conceived specifically for the hi-tech market. This is a critical component of understanding each profile and its relationship to its neighbors.

As to the five categories, Moore described them as follows:

- *Innovators* pursue new technology products aggressively. They sometimes seek them out even before a formal marketing program has been launched. This is because technology is a central interest in their life … At root they are intrigued with any fundamental advance and often make a technology purchase simply for the pleasure of exploring the new device's properties. There are not very many innovators in any given market segment, but winning them over at the outset of a marketing campaign is key nonetheless, because their endorsement reassures the other players in the marketplace that the product does in fact work.

- *Early Adopters,* like innovators, buy into new product concepts very early in their life cycle, but unlike innovators, they are not technologists. Rather they are people who find it easy to imagine, understand, and appreciate the benefits of a new technology, and to relate these potential benefits to their other concerns. Whenever they find a strong match, early adopters are willing to base their buying decisions upon it. Because early adopters do not rely on well-established references in making these buying decisions, they are key to opening up any high-tech market segment.

- The *Early Majority* share some of the early adopters' ability to relate to technology, but ultimately they are driven by a strong sense of practicality. They know that many of these new inventions end up as passing fads, so they are content to wait and see how other people are making out before they buy in themselves. They want to see well-established references before investing substantially. Because there are so many people in this segment – roughly one-third of the whole adoption life cycle – winning their business is key to any substantial profits and growth.

- The *Late Majority* shares all the concerns of the early majority, plus one major additional one: whereas people in the early majority feel able to handle a technology product, should they finally decide to purchase it, members of the late majority are not. As a result, they wait until something has become an established standard, and even then want to see lots of support before they buy, typically from large, well-established companies. Like the early majority, this group comprises about one-third of the total buying population in any given segment. Courting this group is highly profitable, for while profit margins decrease as the products mature, so do the selling costs, and virtually all the R&D costs have been amortized.

- Finally there are the *Laggards.* These people simply don't want anything to do with new technology, for any of a variety of reasons, some personal and some economic. The only time they ever buy a technological product is when it is buried so deep inside another product – the way, say, that a microprocessor is designed into the braking system of a new car – that they don't even know it is there.

Laggards are generally regarded as not worth pursuing on any other basis.

Moore sums them up as follows:

- *Innovators:* the technology enthusiasts
- *Early Adopters:* the visionaries
- *Early Majority:* the pragmatists
- *Late Majority:* the conservatives
- *Laggards:* the skeptics.

These profiles provide the foundation of Moore's second key model, the High-Tech Marketing Model. That model says that the way to develop a high-tech market is to focus initially on the innovators, grow that market, then move on to the early adopters, grow that market, move on to the early majority, and so on through to the late majority, and even possibly to the laggards. Companies, says Moore, need to use each "captured" group as a base for marketing to the next group, i.e. the innovators endorse a product and this becomes an important base from which a company can develop a credible pitch to the early adopters, the endorsement of the early adopters enables a pitch to the early majority, and so on.

It is, says Moore "important to maintain momentum in order to create a bandwagon effect that makes it natural for the next group to want to buy in. Too much of a delay, and the effect would be something like hanging from a motionless vine – nowhere to go but down."

There is another good reason for keeping up the momentum, namely in Moore's words "to take advantage of your day in the sun before the next day renders you obsolete." Portable electric typewriters, for example, were displaced by portable PCs, which in turn may lose out at some point to Internet terminals.

From this notion of having your day in the sun comes the idea of a *window of opportunity* – another of Moore's concepts for which he is rarely credited. If momentum is lost when a window of opportunity presents itself, then the chances are that a company will be overhauled by a competitor, "thereby losing the advantages exclusive to a technology leadership position – specifically, the profit-margin advantage during the middle to late stages, which is the primary source from which high-tech fortunes are made." This is the point at which a product "crosses the chasm" of the book's title.

To summarize, the essence of the High-Tech Marketing Model is a smooth transition through all the stages of the Technology Adoption Life

**Zeitbite**

"In high tech, the good news is that, although we lose our companies with alarming frequency, we keep the people along with the ideas, and so the industry as a whole goes forward vibrantly."

Taken from *Crossing the Chasm*

Cycle. For those companies that get it right, writes Moore, the potential rewards are huge: "What is dazzling about this concept, particularly to those who own equity in a high-tech venture, is its promise of virtual monopoly over a major new market development. If you can get there first, 'catch the curve', and ride it up through the early majority segment, thereby establishing the *de facto* standard, you can get rich very quickly and "own" a highly profitable market for a very long time to come."

## The author

Geoffrey A. Moore is President of The Chasm Group, based in Palo Alto, California. The Chasm Group provides consultancy services to high-tech companies like Hewlett-Packard, Apple, PeopleSoft, AT&T, Oracle, Silicon Graphics and Sybase.

## Sources and further reading

Moore, Geoffrey A. (1999) *Crossing the Chasm: Marketing and Selling Technology Products to Mainstream Customers* (2nd edn), HarperCollins, USA.
The first edition was written in 1990 and published in 1991.

Moore, Geoffrey A. (2000) *Living on the Faultline*, HarperCollins, USA.
Moore's latest book looks at the issue of managing for shareholder value in the age of the Internet. Moore's prediction, and he's been right often enough to merit being taken seriously, is that the next big market is "massive outsourcing that is Web-enabled."

Moore, Geoffrey A. (1995) *Inside the Tornado*, HarperCollins, USA.

Moore, Geoffrey A., Johnson, Paul and Kippola, Tom (1999) *The Gorilla Game*, HarperCollins, USA.
The authors examine what makes a technology company a good investment bet. Being a clear architectural leader in its category is the key, coupled with good underpinning technology and operating practices within the company.

# GEOFF MULGAN

## *Connexity*

### 1997

L anguage lovers among us will be heartened to see that Geoff Mulgan, founder and former director of independent think-tank Demos, has revived an old English word to describe a world that is becoming ever more closely and intricately connected.

"Connexity" describes the interdependence that stems from our all being tied into a global economy, environment, and communication system. For example, by choosing to buy one item of clothes rather than another, we contribute to a process that may ultimately determine whether someone on the other side of the world retains or loses their job; emissions originating in one part of the world can contribute to problems with the ozone layer somewhere else; using the Internet or the mobile phone, we can communicate with others at any time and just about anywhere in the world.

Mulgan believes that this degree of interconnectedness, where we are all joined together physically, psychologically and informationally, brings a host of opportunities and constraints that carry significant implications for governments, organizations, and individuals alike.

By way of response, he argues that, amongst other reforms, the time has come to:

- reshape our institutions to cope with the implications and capabilities of the Internet;
- reshape education to prepare people to make their own decisions and to take responsibility;
- rethink economics – so companies are designed to meet real goals, not just profits – and make firms owned by the people who work for them; and

- persuade government to share responsibility with citizens and to use new forms of democracy like juries and electronic referendums.

However, before tackling these reforms, we need to get to grips with a paradox: despite connexity, human beings have also never been more separate, distanced or distracted. An absolute faith in individual rights and freedoms is a mindset at the heart of the West's world view. We insist on our freedom to choose how to live, who to love, what to consume and what to believe. In economics, the needs and desires of the consumer and the shareholder come first. In politics, the sovereignty of nations remains a fundamental concern. We are not naturally good at, or disposed to, thinking globally.

Mulgan is in no doubt that this tension between freedom and connectedness will have to be resolved, for the two are set on a collision course. He suggests that the only way out of this impasse is to transcend our sense of ourselves as isolated units, and recognize the webs of mutual responsibility in which we live. For although the achievement of much greater freedom is something to be cherished, we can't afford to ignore the consequences, such as environmental decay, social and economic division, dwindling commitment in the home and the workplace, and institutions, including governments, which now seem outdated and inadequate.

Drawing on a wide array of ideas and disciplines – he quotes Charles Darwin, Charles Handy, Thomas Paine, Carl Jung and Nelson Mandela to name only a handful – Mulgan has written a challenging and stimulating book whose only weakness is that it is stronger on analysis, frameworks for thinking about thinking about progress, and bold declarations than it is on suggesting practical ways for individuals and organizations to operate in a connected world.

### Reality Check: just how connected are we?

"At the moment, some of the features of connexity may appear to be relevant only for a privileged minority, and it is true that the thickest connections are experienced only by about a billion people, in North America and Europe, Japan and the tiger economies of East Asia, and in the middle classes of China, India and Latin America. For the rest, more basic needs remain paramount. But even the poorest people on earth share the same climate as the richest, and, looking ahead, few are likely to long remain insulated from the pace of change in technology and culture. In any event, it will be in the poorer areas of the world

that an already densely packed planet is set to double its population
during the course of the next century."

Taken from *Connexity*

## The author

Geoff Mulgan is the founder of London-based independent think-tank
Demos. He was Director of Demos from its creation in 1993 until 1997
when he accepted a policy role within Tony Blair's advisory team. He
is visiting professor at University College London. Mulgan has written
a range of books and pamphlets on broadcasting, telecommunications
and culture. He also contributes regularly to the *Guardian* and the
*Independent*.

## Sources and further reading

Mulgan, Geoff (1997) *Connexity*, Chatto and Windus, UK.
The Demos Website is located at www.demos.co.uk

Senge, Peter (1990) *The Fifth Discipline*, Business Books, USA.
Those wanting to explore the concept of connexity in a practical and
tangible way may find the section in this book on systems thinking
helpful. The 70 pages that Senge devotes to the subject represents an
excellent generalist introduction to the main concepts of what is a core
skill in a globalized, networked economy.

# JOHN NAISBITT

## *Megatrends*

### 1982

T o read *Megatrends* again is to be reminded of just how profound and wide ranging technological change has been over the past 20 years, the last five or so in particular. In his book, John Naisbitt identified ten "critical restructurings." that he believed would shape our lives. While some of his predictions have proved astonishingly accurate, others have been wide of the mark or of diminishing significance. Let's look at the ten areas Naisbitt highlighted:

1   "Although we continue to think we live in an industrial society, we have in fact changed to an economy based on the creation and distribution of information." *Through a 21st century lens, this statement appears self-evident. Twenty years ago, when the working population in the West was dominated by office workers and the manufacturing industry, it was a much bolder assertion.*

2   "We are moving in the dual directions of high tech/high touch, matching each new technology with a compensatory human response ... The acceleration of technological progress has created an urgent need for a counter ballast for high touch experiences ... High touch is about getting back to a human scale ... Also, remember that high-tech/high-touch isn't an either/or decision. You can't stop technological progress, but by the same token, you can hardly go wrong with a high-touch response. Give out your home phone number. Send a hand-written letter. FedEx has all the reliability and efficiency of modern electronics, but its success is built on a form of high touch: hand delivery." *Naisbitt has returned to the high tech/high touch from time to time, most recently in his book* Hightech Hightouch, *published in 1999. Because of the relentless pace of technological progress since* Megatrends *was first published, and the risks of*

*alienation posed by aspects of the IT revolution, this theme is now more relevant than ever.*

3 "No longer do we have the luxury of operating within an isolated, self-sufficient, national economic system; we must now acknowledge that we are part of a global economy ... The bigger the world economy, the more powerful its smallest player." *The new economy is demonstrably a global economy. Thanks to Internet technology, a one-person global business is both technically feasible and a practical reality*

4 "We are restructuring from a society run by short-term considerations and rewards in favor of dealing with things in much longer-term time frames." *Despite one or two counter-examples (see* Built to Last *by Collins and Porras or* The Living Company *by Arie de Geus), short-termism seems just as rife today – both ecologically and organizationally.*

5 "In cities and states, in small organizations and subdivisions, we have rediscovered the ability to act innovatively and to achieve results from the bottom up." *There is some evidence that grass roots groups – sometimes using the Internet to co-ordinate efforts and to disseminate information instantaneously – are having some success. Within organizations, a combination of delayering and empowerment initiatives has devolved greater responsibility to those in the frontline.*

6 "We are shifting from institutional help to more self-reliance in all aspects of our lives." *With the "job for life" available now to only a select few, there is now a greater emphasis on individuals needing to invest effort in maintaining their employability. Internet services, such as on-line banking, give the customer far greater control over processes than ever before.*

7 "We are discovering that the framework of representative democracy has become obsolete in an era of instantaneously shared information." *Despite the current debate in the UK about the political influence wielded by spin doctors on the government payroll, there is no substantial evidence that much has yet changed.*

8 "We are giving up our dependence on hierarchical structures in favor of informal networks. This will be especially important to the business community." *Mixed signals here: on the one hand, technology has enabled networks to develop (with suppliers, between competitors, internally, globally) in a variety of ways; on the other hand, there is some evidence that hierarchy is hardwired into human behavior.*

9 "More Americans are living in the South and West leaving behind the old industrial cities of the North." *Silicon Valley has grown in significance since the 1980s, and US employment patterns support the*

*assertion to an extent. Compared to the other nine "restructurings" though, and in the context of a global economy, this now seems like a curiously parochial point for Naisbitt to make.*

10  "From a narrow either/or society with a limited range of personal choices, we are exploding into a free-wheeling multiple option society." *Perhaps for some, but certainly not for most people.*

It's tempting to measure the value of *Megatrends* purely by the extent to which its predictions have come to pass. On that basis, Naisbitt gave back in 1982 an impressively accurate foretaste of the new economy (if we define it loosely as the combination of technology, e-business, free agent working, and globalization).

Critics of futurologists say that predicting the future is a sterile act that in itself makes nothing happen, any more than the act of betting influences which horse is first past the post. That assessment seems too harsh. Louis Pasteur once said that chance favors only the prepared mind. By that token, characterizing the future helps in some measure to invent it.

## What is high tech/high touch?

"It is a human lens.

"It is embracing technology that preserves our humanness and rejecting technology that intrudes upon it. It is recognizing that technology is an integral part of the evolution of culture, the creative product of our imaginations, our dreams and aspirations – and that the desire to create new technologies is fundamentally instinctive. But is also recognizing that art, story, play, religion, nature, and time are equal partners in the evolution of technology because they nourish the soul and fulfil its yearnings. It is expressing what it means to be human and employing technology fruitfully in that expression. It's appreciating life and accepting death. It is knowing when we should push back on technology, in our work and our lives, to affirm our humanity. It is understanding that technology zealots are as short-sighted as technology bashers. It is creating significant paths for our lives, without fear of new technology or fear of falling behind it. It is recognizing that at its best, technology supports and improves human life; at its worse, it alienates, isolates, distorts, and destroys. It is questioning what place technology should have in our lives and what place it should have in society. It is consciously choosing to employ technology when it adds value to human lives. It is learning how to live

> **Zeitbite**
>
> "The new source of power is not money in the hands of a few but information in the hands of many."
>
> John Naisbitt

as human beings in a technologically dominated time. It is knowing when simulated experiences add value to human life. It is recognizing when to avoid the layers of distractions and distance technology affords us. It is recognizing when technology is not neutral. It is knowing when to unplug and when to plug in. It is appropriate human scale.

"High Tech/High Touch is enjoying the fruits of technological advancements and having it truly sit well with our god, our church, or our spiritual beliefs. It is understanding technology through the human lens of play, time, religion, and art."

Taken from *High Tech High Touch* by John Naisbitt

## The author

John Naisbitt (born 1930) worked as an executive with IBM and Eastman Kodak, and has been a distinguished international fellow at the Institute of Strategic and International Studies in Kuala Lumpur. He is a futurologist whose books have sold in their millions. Naisbitt was educated at Cornell.

His most recent book, *High Tech High Touch* (written in collaboration with Nana Naisbitt and Douglas Phillips returns to one of – technology and our search for meaning

## Sources and further reading

Naisbitt, John (1982) *Megatrends*, Warner Books, USA.

Naisbitt, John, Naisbitt, Nana & Philips, Douglas (1999) *High Tech High Touch*, Nicholas Brealey.

Gibson, Rowan (ed.) (1996) *Rethinking the Future*, Nicholas Brealey, UK.

De Geus, Arie (1997) *The Living Company*, Nicholas Brealey, UK.

# NICHOLAS NEGROPONTE

## *Being Digital*

## 1995

A founder and regular contributor to *Wired* magazine, Nicholas Negroponte is perhaps the world's best-known multi-media watcher and commentator. *Being Digital* was a bestseller when it first came out, and deservedly since Negroponte was one of the first and certainly one of the most readable trackers of the birth of new media.

The book consists of what he calls a "re-purposing" of many of the themes first visited in his monthly *Wired* column in the early to mid-nineties. This is both a strength and a weakness. On the positive side, the book fizzes with practical insights into the future of communications. On the other hand, his columns occasionally seem less "re-purposed" than repackaged.

The average length of the sections is two to three pages, which is generally long enough to get over a couple of snappy points but allows little opportunity for considered reflection of big-picture issues. Negroponte seems content to describe rather than to analyze: in the fast-changing world of multimedia, this is understandable but as a result the book has not aged well in the five years since its first publication.

Although the book sports a five-page epilogue – and that's expansive by Negroponte's standards – what the book lacks is an incisive conclusion bringing together the key themes that Negroponte touches on but never really makes explicit.

### Reality check: the dangers of separating text from context

A Trip Report from Portugal by Paul Duguid.
"I was working in an archive of a 250-year-old business, reading

## The difference between bits and atoms

"The best way to appreciate the merits and consequences of being digital is to reflect on the difference between atoms and bits. While we are undoubtedly in an information age, most information is delivered to us in the form of atoms: newspapers, magazines and books ... Our economy may be moving toward an information economy, but we measure trade and we write our balance sheets with atoms in mind."

Taken from *Being Digital*

"I comprehend something best when I can explain it in a few simple words. Describing the world in terms of 'bits and atoms,' as I did in my book *Being Digital*, provided those words. In fact, as a description of the digital world, the 'bits and atoms' distinction has improved, not weakened, over time. People quickly grasp the consequences of those 1s and 0s that have no weight, no size, no shape, and no color, and can travel at the speed of light.

"Just to name a few: your marginal cost to make more bits is zero. You need no inventory. You can sell them and keep them for yourself at the same time. The originals and the copies are indistinguishable. They don't stop at customs. Governments cannot tell where they are. Regulators cannot determine their appropriate jurisdiction. The global marketplace for bits welcomes even the smallest company."

From Negroponte's foreword to *Unleashing the Killer App* by Downes and Mui

correspondence from about the time of the American Revolution. Incoming letters were stored in wooden boxes about the size of a standard Styrofoam picnic cooler, each containing a fair portion of dust as old as the letters. As opening a letter triggered a brief asthmatic attack, I wore a scarf tied over my nose and mouth. Despite my bandit's attire, my nose ran, my eyes wept, and I coughed, wheezed, and snorted. I longed for a digital system that would hold the information from the letters and leave paper and dust behind.

"One afternoon, another historian came to work on a similar box. He read barely a word. Instead, he picked out bundles of letters and, in a move that sent my sinuses into shock, ran each letter beneath his nose and took a deep breath, at times almost inhaling the letter itself but always getting a good dose of dust. Sometimes, after a particularly profound sniff, he would open the letter, glance at it briefly, make a note and move on. Choking behind my mask, I asked him what he was doing. He was, he told me, a medical historian. (A profession to avoid if you have asthma.) He was documenting outbreaks of cholera. When that disease occurred in a town in the eighteenth century, all letters from that town were disinfected with vinegar to prevent the disease from spreading. By sniffing for the faint traces of vinegar that survived 250 years and noting the date and source of the letters, he was able to chart the progress of cholera outbreaks.

"His research threw new light on the letter I was reading. Now cheery letters telling customers and creditors that all was well, business thriving, and the future rosy read a little differently if a whiff of vinegar came off the page. Then the correspondent's cheeriness might be an act to prevent a collapse of business confidence unaware that he or she would be betrayed by a scent of vinegar."

Taken from *The Social Life of Information*
by John Seely Brown and Paul Duguid

## The author

Nicholas Negroponte is the Director of the Media Laboratory of the Massachusetts Institute of Technology, and is widely regarded as one of the world's leading experts on multimedia. He is also a founder of *Wired* magazine, to which he still regularly contributes.

## Sources and further reading

Negroponte, Nicholas (1995) *Being digital*, Knopf, USA.

To track current developments in new media technology, the two best sources are probably *Wired* and *Red Herring*. Both magazines are published monthly.

# JEFF PAPOWS

## *Enterprise.com*

### 1999

I n *Enterprise.com*, Jeff Papows offers an incisive vision of the technology revolution, and a wide-ranging exploration of the networked world we live in. As CEO of Lotus – one of the best known and most progressive software companies – he has a decent vantage point from which to survey developments to date, which he describes as just "really just a warm-up for the far greater changes to come."

Businesses are going to have to change – and change radically – in order to compete effectively in the Web-based era: but the good news, says Papows, is that technological advances are opening as many windows of opportunity as they are threatening to close obsolete and outmoded ones. In his book, he gives some good, if by now familiar, examples of how technology is influencing the way businesses operate:

- Federal Express putting up a Web server in 1994 to provide public access to their internal package tracking database and then finding that many of their customers preferred tracking their deliveries on-line.
- On-line book retailer Amazon.com spawning an entirely new approach to retailing.
- Customer service is changing; enquiries and orders handled over the telephone today will soon be managed over the Internet as a matter of course, at a considerably lower cost. In the US, it costs $1 to process a typical bank transaction in the conventional way; on the Web, the cost is just one cent.

But he goes well beyond these examples of technology being applied creatively. What interests Papows is the future, a future in which, for example, organizations will have to come fully to terms with the dynamics of a borderless, 24-hour world. He sees the inevitable rise of the "market-facing enterprise," with all relationships enhanced and even defined through technology. "The Web enables a company's technology systems to interface directly with any and all customers, regardless of time or location, potentially eliminating many face to face and telephone based intermediaries," he writes. The focus will move from inside to outside the organization to the vast network of suppliers, distributors, customers and partners who are vital to success.

Papows is astute enough to recognize that the future of information technology is relatively easy to predict compared to the many complex social, economic, cultural, and political variables that affect business evolution. We expect continuing powerful advances in technology – most of the other factors are far less predictable.

That said, for information technology to reach its full potential, many obstacles must be resolved in a timely and predictable manner. The greatest risks and challenges that lie ahead can, he writes, be divided into the following four areas:

1   *Technological and human limits.* "It's nearly impossible to eliminate the risk that technology itself might not be able to deliver on the many promises it is making. Similarly, the demands of ever more sophisticated systems might one day outstrip the skills and talents of available workers."

2   *Failed standards.* "Even if the technological capacity exists, a real risk remains that today's rising levels of product inter-operability will prove a temporary illusion. The IT industry has yet to prove in a systemic sense that its particular style of competition can sustain a meaningful "open standards" process. The evidence of the last two years in this regard has been positive. But with the experience of the preceding two decades, there is every reason to be concerned that the industry dynamic could shift back to the direction of internecine warfare."

3   *Lack of demand.* "It's also perfectly possible that no matter what technologies and standards emerge, two further problems could arise: businesses might decide that there are limits to the value of automation, or consumers might decide that on-line services are simply not all that compelling. My personal sense on both counts is that the risk is fairly low; but with all our momentum and influence, it's critical that we never forget that it is the customer we must endeavor to satisfy, not ourselves."

4   *Government intervention.* "For reasons of commerce, culture, politics, fairness, and security, some governments may seek to block largely unfettered use of the Internet. In this realm of Internet governance, I can foresee two main problems: restrictions on the flow of commerce and restrictions on the flow of information."

*Enterprise.com* goes beyond the traditional boundaries of business, although in truth not very far. There are valuable insights into the full scope of emerging technologies – and into their role in the information economy – and into the challenges created as governments, businesses and individuals clash over such issues as privacy, regulation, encryption and common standards – but nothing earth-shattering. Papows gives us a detailed and thoughtful analysis of where business is headed over the next few years, but the book lacks sparkle and originality. There's nothing wrong in what Papows is saying, and as a major player in the software world, his views do carry considerable weight. Nonetheless, it is difficult to get excited about *Enterprise.com*. File under: "Another CEO, another business book."

## The author

Jeff Papows is President and CEO of Lotus Development Corporation based in Cambridge, Massachusetts. A prominent voice in the information technology industry, he is a frequent commentator in the business media and a regular keynote speaker at conferences. He holds a PhD.

## Sources and further reading

Papows, Jeff (1999) *Enterprise.com*, Nicholas Brealey, USA.

# DON PEPPERS & MARTHA ROGERS

## *Enterprise One-to-One*

## 1997

M ost companies, and certainly those with an intuitive grasp of how the new economy is unfolding, know that customers are no longer passive recipients of a service or purchasers of a product. Customers tell you what they want, and expect you to fit around their needs and circumstances. They expect you to remember them. And as for the idea that, once with you, they will stay for life, the 21st-century customer's attitude is "If you want loyalty, get a dog."

Against this backdrop, companies are grasping that they need to listen to customers far more attentively and, above all else, recognize that customers come in packages of one.

In *Enterprise One-to-One*, Don Peppers and Martha Rogers explore what companies need to do to thrive in this new competitive environment, and offer some practical tools and approaches to help them embrace the world of mass customization and customer relationship management.

At its most basic, the 1:1 enterprise must be able to treat different customers differently. Actions toward an individual customer need to be based explicitly on their particular needs. This requires the company and the customer to collaborate and determine jointly what the appropriate product or service is for that customer.

A key challenge for companies is to work out how integrate its actual production and service delivery processes with the feedback it receives by interacting with specific, individual customers. To this end, say the authors, information technology is making three important new capabilities available to businesses:

- powerful databases allow the company to tell their customers apart and remember them individually;
- interactivity means the customer can now talk to the company directly; and
- mass customization technology enables businesses to customize products and services as a matter of routine.

But the challenge of putting in place a successful mass customization program goes far deeper than buying the right IT solution. Peppers and Rogers highlight the example of telephone company MCI who launched a customer retention program that failed – despite quantifiable progress – because of organizational conflict and cultural resistance. the program was eventually abandoned because, amongst other things, it conflicted with existing management incentives, which were based on customer acquisition rates but not retention.

Assuming a company can harness the information technology needed and put in place an appropriately skilled and motivated work-force, there still needs to be a well-developed and executed marketing strategy to ensure that, alongside the needs of individual customers, that the company's financial needs are being met. There is no corporate merit to brilliantly serving inherently unprofitable customers and going into receivership.

From a strategic and financial perspective, therefore, companies need to use information generated about customers to identify their value to the business. The authors write that "a customer's lifetime value (LTV) will depend largely on how long the customer remains loyal, and even small increases in the rate of customer retention add significantly to LTV." However, knowing what different customers need involves much more than simply keeping a record of *what* they've bought. Companies need increasingly to know *why*. This is important because two customers might buy the same product for quite different reasons; knowing the thinking behind the purchase gives a company a much better chance of securing future business.

While customers with the highest lifetime values are the ones you most want to nurture and retain, Peppers and Rogers suggest that second-tier customers – customers who don't have as high an actual valuation – are likely to have the most potential for growth. Keeping a first-tier customer will usually involve different strategies from those needed for growing a second-tier customer. At the other end of the spectrum, most companies also have a bottom rung of customers who are, for all practical purposes, of no value to the company. Shaking off these customers is not easy: taking positive action to do so can attract

## Zeitbite: one-to-one thinking

"When you subscribe to a new magazine, the first year might cost $35.90 but the second year the price is $75.90. Why? Because presumably you like the magazine. Charging regular customers more is a natural consequence of trying to acquire new customers by using discounts, and virtually every business tries to do it. But by tailoring a product to a customer's individual specifications, and then constantly upgrading the product to match the customer's needs better and better, the enterprise can establish a Learning Relationship with the customer. Over time, the enterprise not only makes the customer more and more loyal, it increases its own value to that customer – as every interaction leads to a better tailored service or product."

Taken from *Enterprise One-to-One*

negative publicity as Barclays Bank discovered when it closed down a number of its rural branches in the UK in the early part of 2000.

Although the authors identify some practical "quick wins" that a company can enact, becoming a 1:1 enterprise is not something that can simply be added to the management toolkit like one more technique for improving quality, reducing cost, or raising productivity. Rather, the authors write, "it represents a fundamental change in philosophy and strategy – a change in the dynamics of competition. A true 1:1 marketing philosophy can't be implemented without integrating it into the entire organization. The firm must embrace significant change, affecting virtually every department, division, officer and employee, every product, and every function."

They go on to identify four steps involved in making the 1:1 journey – visioning, organizing, measuring, and transitioning – and offer some hints about each stage.

Three years or so after its publication, *Enterprise One-to-One* remains about the best book around how customers and companies will interact in the new economy. It's a book that achieves the rare distinction of offering both a strategic perspective and a set of practical tools and tips and being absolutely convincing at both levels. Most critical of all, they leave the reader in no doubt that, just as Henry Ford's approach to mass production transformed manufacturing in the 20th century, so mass customization is set to be just as significant in the 21st.

**Zeitbite**

"Speed and good communications are essential if mass customization is to work. Get them right, and another prize is yours. In Henry Ford's day, Ford made the car and the customer paid for it. in Michael Dell's day, the customer pays for the computer and then Dell makes it."

*Economist*, April 1, 2000

## The authors

Don Peppers and Martha Rogers are authors of a number of best-selling business books, most of them based around their concept of "one-to-one marketing." Their company, the Peppers and Rogers Group, offers consulting and training in customer relationship management, and was recently included in the Inc 500 list of the fastest growing companies in the US.

## Sources and further reading

Peppers, Don, & Rogers, Martha (1997) *Enterprise One to One: Tools for Competing in the Interactive Age*, Doubleday, USA.

Peppers, Don, Rogers, Martha and Dorf, Bob (1999) *The One to One Fieldbook*, Doubleday, USA.
Described as "a complete toolkit for companies implementing customer relationship programs," *The One to One Fieldbook* is jam-packed with marketing concepts, case studies, checklists, quotes, and so on. On top of that, tucked into the book is a card containing a special individual access code to the authors' Website, in which readers can find yet more spreadsheets, checklists and self assessment tools. The book is ideal for those looking for plenty of stimulation and ideas, but anybody looking for a more considered appraisal of the topic would be better off going for *Enterprise One-to-One*.

Peppers, Don and Rogers, Martha (2000) *The One to One Manager*, Doubleday, USA.
This book explores the actual management issues involved in implementing Customer Relationship Management (CRM) initiatives. Some very informative case studies are featured.

# TOM PETERS

## *The Brand You 50*

## 1999

W | ith the publication of *In Search of Excellence* in 1982, Tom Peters and co-author Bob Waterman changed the way organizations thought about themselves. Notions of embracing a paradoxical world of constant change, of providing exemplary customer service and of the need for high-speed response are now mainstream corporate thinking, but during the mid-1980s, when he was at the peak of his fame, the challenge laid down by Peters was enormous.

Even so, *In Search of Excellence* did have some gaps in its thinking, as Peters acknowledged in an interview published in Information Strategy magazine in 1998:

> *Interviewer:* You published your first best-seller, *In Search of Excellence*, almost exactly fifteen years ago. What would be different if you were writing it today?
> *Tom Peters:* I would have focused a lot more on the information technology. It still amazes me after fifteen years that I'm seen as a radical because, when I look back I would guess that 90% of my errors have been errors of conservatism, not radicalism. But I guess it was a pretty radical message for the time, in a world that wasn't ready for globalism or the value of information. What I did focus on a lot in that book was the importance of pleasing customers. Even that was considered radical back then.

In recent years, Peters has focussed increasingly on how changes at a corporate, national and global level impact on the nature of work for us as individuals. It is a topical theme that takes a variety of guises

– knowledge workers making a living out of Charles Leadbeater's "thin air"; McKinsey warning its clients that the biggest challenge for companies is "the war for talent"; Charles Handy's "portfolio workers"; Harriet Rubin's "soloists"; business magazines like *Fast Company* devoted to Me Inc. or me.com and full of advice on "why it pays to quit," how you should be hotdesking with colleagues, telecommuting from home, and generally reconsidering your whole future.

In August 1997, Peters contributed an article to *Fast Company* titled "The brand called you: you can't move up if you don't stand out." It's a brilliant synthesis of economic, marketing and business themes that ends with a stark conclusion:

"It's this simple: you are a brand. You are in charge of your brand. There is no single path to success. And there is no one right way to create the brand called You. Except this: Start today. Or else."

Two years later Peters expanded the article into book form with *The Brand You 50*.

Reading the book for the first time reminded me of a conversation I had 15 years ago. A friend of mine was telling me that a Tom Peters book should never be read from cover to cover but rather should be dipped into briefly and at random, studied for meaning, and then stored away in a dark room until a further dose was required. "It's like the sun," I remember him saying, "you need the illumination but it's dangerous to stare at it for any length of time." If Tom's prose style seemed disjointed in the eighties, heaven knows what my old chum would make of *The Brand You 50*, a business book written entirely in soundbites.

Underpinning *The Brand You 50* is Tom's passionate belief that the individual has become the fundamental unit in the new economy. The book consists of, in his words, "fifty ways to transform yourself from an employee into a brand that shouts distinction, commitment and passion."

Stripped to their essence – decide what you want to do, and then do it obsessively – many of the ideas in the book are valid but, two years on from his *Fast Company* article, no longer particularly original. Perhaps that explains why Peters takes his trademark use of hyperbole to new levels – if the quality of his thinking doesn't persuade you, then the sheer volume and intensity of his scatter-gun sentences might. But actually it's the language that undermines his message. You may just about cope with statements like "CLUTTER KILLS WOW" being sprinkled throughout the book. However, any book that asks the reader to repeat after the author "I am as cool as the coolness of the dudes/dudettes I associate with" invites ridicule.

Maybe Peters won't mind this sort of reaction – he has after all made a career out of provoking his audience. However, times have moved on and Peters the one-time Heretic, presenting unpalatable truths to unreceptive executives, has turned into – in this book at least – Peters the Loudmouth with little to say.

### Tom Peters says goodbye to the job for life

"It's over. Praise God its over. The world in which 'we' – the best and the brightest, the college kids – depended on 'them,' the Big Companies to 'guide' (micromanage! dictate! control!) 'our' careers. Alas my Dad was no more than an indentured servant to the Baltimore Gas & Electric Company for 41 years. Same door. West Lexington Street. Day after day. Month after month. Year after year. Decade after decade. It was no way to live, if living it were. But 'It' is finished. Kaput."

Source: *The Brand You 50*

### Reality check

"Most people on the political left – particularly in Europe – share Peters' fundamental analysis while drawing the opposite conclusions. They believe that the very forces that Peters celebrates – technology, globalization, the shift toward services – are breaking down the old social contract, leaving workers at the mercy of a new and ruthless variety of capitalism."

Source: *Future Perfect*, by Stan Davis

## The author

Tom Peters is probably the best known management guru in the world. Other gurus like Peter Drucker have a faithful following but nobody can touch Peters for penetration of the management consciousness. It was while they both worked at McKinsey in the 1970s that Peters met Bob Waterman, and it was their collaboration on *In Search of Excellence* that propelled Peters onto the international stage in 1982. Peters was and remains an outstanding speaker and communicator. His disingenuous description of himself as a regular guy who "just talks about stuff I've seen" underplays his unique ability to survey the business world, synthesize what he sees, and then present his findings in an accessible, vibrant and provocative way. Peters is the founder of the Tom Peters Company, with offices in Palo Alto, Boston, Chicago and London. He and his family live on a farm in Vermont and an island off the Massachusetts coast, thanks to the information revolution. His Website address is www.tompeters.com and he can be contacted at tom@tompeters.com

## Sources and further reading

Peters, Tom (1999) *The Brand You 50*, Knopf, USA.

Peters, Tom (1997) "The brand called you," *Fast Company*, August–September.

Peters, Tom and Waterman, Robert (1982) *In Search of Excellence*, HarperCollins, USA.
In *In Search of Excellence*, Tom Peters and co-author Bob Waterman identified eight characteristics of excellent companies. Although they subsequently acknowledged that their recipe was incomplete, many of the individual elements remain valid. In particular their view that management is about taking action – two of their eight characteristics are Bias to Action and Hands-on Management – and getting things done still hold good.

Crainer, Stuart (1997) *Corporate Man to Corporate Skunk – a Biography of Tom Peters*, Capstone, UK.
For those interested in Tom Peters, Stuart Crainer's biography captures the man, his method and his impact on management thinking admirably. The book focuses on Peters' public life, hardly touching on his private affairs (a multi-millionaire who has been married four times). In doing so, it gives a clear and balanced appraisal of a man who is unquestionably a business phenomenon.

*Wired* magazine, December 1997
Peters shares his thinking on a range of topics in a four-page interview with Kevin Kelly.

# TOM PETZINGER

## *The New Pioneers*

### 1999

T homas Petzinger spent 20 years as a journalist at the *Wall Street Journal*, before leaving in 2000 to set up his own business. His last four years at the paper were spent covering a rich variety of business stories, and conducting hundreds of face-to-face interviews with successful small business owners, which he featured in a his weekly column called "The Front Lines."

In *The New Pioneers*, Petzinger describes how many of these interviews produced "disorienting reporting experiences" that turned traditional business thinking on its head. People just didn't do what the business books said they ought to do; more often than not, they were doing the complete opposite. And yet they were achieving astonishing success. This led Petzinger to conclude in his final Front Lines column that "in the new economy, everyone is an entrepreneur"

This is how Petzinger characterizes new pioneers:

> "Today's pioneers have embarked on a new frontier, some in search of riches, others in search of freedom, all in search of the new. Unlike the West of old this frontier is not one of place. It is a frontier of technologies, ideas, and values. The new pioneers celebrate individuality over conformity among their employees and customers alike. They deploy technology to distribute rather than consolidate authority and creativity. They compete through resilience instead of resistance, through adaptation instead of control. In a time of dizzying complexity and change, they realize that tightly drawn strategies become brittle while shared purpose endures. Capitalism, in short, is merging with humanism."

**Zeitbite**

"In 1962, while walking around the production factory at Non-Linear Systems with his tape recorder in his hand, Abraham Maslow dictated the following entry: 'The most valuable one hundred people to bring into a deteriorating society ... would not be one hundred chemists, or politicians, or professors, or engineers, but rather one hundred entrepreneurs.' In Maslow's time, entrepreneurs were much fewer in number, and almost none worked in major corporations. Today entrepreneurs abound, not just in small business but across the landscape of the corporate world. They have brought us this far, and they will take us further still."

Taken from *The New Pioneers*

*The New Pioneers*, then, is about a revolution that Petzinger believes is quietly reshaping the face of American business and creating an opportunity-rich economy. This revolution is not to be found in the headline-grabbing mega-mergers, takeovers, downsizing, fiscal crises, or bust-ups that dominate the front pages of the financial press; rather these changes are visible in the spectacular success enjoyed by a growing number of small- and medium-sized firms.

At the heart of these firms' success, he argues, is an entrepreneurial outlook that is team- rather than self-centered. An open, selfless organization is not only good for the business, but also good for all involved, both inside and outside. Such an organization needs people who are individually passionate about what they do but who use all of their resources for the good of the team and the wider company.

Petzinger puts forward a compelling case for small and medium-sized businesses being the engine room of a new economy more often characterized as being populated by mega-corporations at one end of the scale or tiny start-ups or the other – what Charles Handy has called the world of elephants and fleas. Petzinger's focus on this middle group amounts to a revisionist statement.

At a deeper level, he is arguing for a fundamental shift in our collective thinking about the nature of organizations. Few people wake up on a Monday morning positively enthused about the prospect of going into work. And yet Petzinger has uncovered hundreds of small companies where people have a genuine desire to belong and to contribute, where individual capability is harnessed to a collective potential to create astonishing results.

Can small and medium-sized businesses retain this quality as they enjoy success and grow larger? Is big automatically bad? It would have been fascinating to see Petzinger really getting to grips with these questions.

Perhaps it is being churlish to criticize minor omissions when Petzinger gives us so much. *The New Pioneers* proves its own hypothesis, that business with a human face can work as well if not better than more traditional approaches, brilliantly, employing a compelling mix of anecdotes and analysis. There is, though, just a nagging feeling that a little less story-telling and a bit more analysis and reflection might have made this an absolute classic.

### Reality check: technology and the middleman – the best of friends

"As the theory goes, information technology puts producers directly in contact with their customers, collapsing the distribution chain, wiping out all those who have made their living by taking orders or breaking big lots into smaller lots. A spooky technical term has been coined for this process: disintermediation. 'Middleman functions between consumers and producers are being eliminated,' the futurist Don Tapscott wrote in the influential best-seller *The Digital Economy*. Patrick McGovern, chairman of International Data Group, the world's largest high-tech publisher, is even more dour. 'The intermediary is doomed,' he wrote in *Forbes ASAP*. 'Technology strips him of effectiveness.'

"I think the doomsayers are flat wrong. Information technology is the friend of the middleman. Technology wipes out inefficiency, it's true and thank goodness. But that is hardly the only way it adds value. Technology makes possible the integration of services on the smallest of scales. It has created a whole category of firms called 'infomediaries,' turning teachers and grad students from Stanford and Carnegie Mellon into overnight millionaires. Technology explains how a single entrepreneur can create Amazon.com, the world's largest bookstore, on little more than a great idea."

Taken from *The New Pioneers*

## The author

Thomas Petzinger worked at the *Wall Street Journal* for over 20 years, before leaving in 2000, holding a variety of positions. For four years, he wrote a weekly column called "The Front Lines." He is a graduate of the Medill School of Journalism at Northwestern University. He recently created LaunchCyte Inc., a small business incubator based in Pittsburgh, Pennsylvania. of which he is Chairman and CEO

He is author of *Hard Landing: the Epic Contest for Power and Profits that Plunged the Airlines into Chaos* (Times Books, 1997)

## Sources and further reading

Petzinger, Thomas (1999) *The New Pioneers: Men and Women who are Transforming the Workplace and Marketplace*, Simon and Schuster, USA.
Petzinger can be contacted by e-mail at tom@petzinger.com
The *Petzinger Report* newsletter can be found at www.petzinger.com

# B. JOSEPH PINE & JAMES H. GILMORE

## The Experience Economy

## 1999

W hy does a cup of coffee cost more from a trendy café than it does from the street vendor or when made at home? Partly it's because of the inherent costs involved, but more significant is the nature of the experience and the value attached to it. So say Pine and Gilmore, who begin this fascinating book by taking the reader through the following life story of a coffee bean:

> "Companies that harvest coffee or trade it on the futures market receive – at the time of this writing – a little more than $1 per pound, which translates into one or two cents a cup. When a manufacturer grinds, packages, and sells those same beans in a grocery store, turning them into a good, the price to a consumer jumps to between 5 and 25 cents a cup (depending on brand and package size). Brew the ground beans in a run-of-the-mill diner, corner coffee shop, or bodega and that service now sells for 50 cents to a dollar per cup. So depending on what a business does with it, coffee can be any of three economic offerings – commodity, good, or service – with three distinct ranges of value customers attach to the offering. But wait: serve that same coffee in a five-star restaurant or espresso bar, where the ordering, creation, and consumption of the cup embodies a heightened ambience or sense of theatre, and consumers gladly pay anywhere from $2 to $5 for each cup. Businesses that ascend to this fourth level of value establish a distinctive experience that envelops the purchase of coffee, increasing its value (and therefore its price) by two orders of magnitude over the original commodity."

The coffee bean's journey from commodity, to good, to service, and finally to experience carries a telling moral: the most obvious and significant source of added value in this whole journey is the point at which the offering becomes an experience for the consumer.

And it's this "fourth level of value" that is the focus of *The Experience Economy*. It is at the experience level that companies have their biggest opportunity to distinguish themselves from their rivals.

The authors hold up Disney as a model provider of experiences. Disney's success, they suggest, can be attributed to the company's ability to sell indelible impressions, engage the senses to facilitate escapism, and create memories.

At the heart of success, say Pine and Gilmore, is a process that delivers a consistent, positive and memorable experience for the customer. They identify five design principles involved in creating a memorable experience:

1   *Theme the experience.* Create a consistent and well-defined theme, one that resonates throughout the entire experience. Eat at the Hard Rock Café or TGI Fridays and you instantly know what to expect when you walk through the door.

2   *Harmonize impressions with positive cues.* While the theme is the foundation of the experience, impressions are the "takeaways" that fulfil the theme. To create the desired impressions, companies must introduce cues that affirm the nature of the experience to the customer. As the authors put it: "Even the smallest cue can aid the creation of a unique experience. When the restaurant host says 'Your table is ready,' no particular cue is given. But when a Rainforest Café host declares, "Your adventure is about to begin." it sets the scene for something special.

3   *Eliminate negative cues.* Crabby staff, long queues, unpleasant environments, intrusive announcements, etc. Unfortunately, the easiest way to turn a service into an experience is to provide poor service – thus creating, to quote the authors, "a memorable encounter of the unpleasant kind."

4   *Mix in memorabilia.* Postcards, T-shirts and so on provide a physical reminder of the experience, and might influence the customer to repeat the experience or, failing that, to share stories about their good experience with friends and colleagues.

5   *Engage the five senses.* The more senses are engaged, the more memorable the experience

The authors warn that these principles do not repeal the laws of supply and demand. An overpriced experience will struggle to attract repeat custom, no matter how well it is delivered. Likewise, overcapacity will see pressure on demand, pricing or both. Nonetheless, they believe that a growth in the experience economy is inevitable, mainly because it represents the best opportunity for a company really to distinguish itself in the eyes of its customers.

Though repetitious and at times verging on the metaphysical, *The Experience Economy* is crammed with illustrations and intriguing insights. From a new economy perspective, it would have been interesting to hear something from the authors about how the experience economy might operate in the on-line world; they do seem to have spent a lot of time in theme parks and restaurants, where the theatricality of experience shows through very easily. That said, Pine and Gilmore offer us another lens through which to view the future of commerce, and that in itself has value.

## The authors

B. Joseph Pine II and James H. Gilmore are co-founders of Strategic Horizons LLP, a consultancy that aims to explore the frontiers of business and to help senior executives see the world differently.

## Sources and further reading

Pine, B. Joseph, and Gilmore, James (1999) *The Experience Economy: Goods and Services are No Longer Enough*, Harvard Business School Press, USA.

Pine, B. Joseph, and Gilmore, James (1998) Welcome to the experience economy, *Harvard Business Review*, July–August.
This article gives a good overview of the topic and probably covers it in enough depth for most people.

# DAVID S. POTTRUCK & HARRY PEARCE

## *Clicks and Mortar*

## 2000

A t a time when Internet businesses all have access to similar technology, and when the models for on-line businesses are such that they can be copied readily, often within a matter of days, how can they achieve a sustainable advantage over their rivals? The answer, say Pottruck and Moore, lies in that often overlooked resource – people. Not just ordinary people, but those with passion.

Passionate companies have cultures that are intentionally created and sustained, and which unequivocally support individual contribution, teamwork, and risk-taking. Business practices in passionate organizations are anchored in the principles that helped the company become successful in the first place. Because of this, passionate companies are more likely to have on board passionate leaders who are themselves driven by a strong set of values, coupled with a genuine desire for their organization and the people who work there to succeed.

Pottruck and Moore's advocacy of passion is not simply the result of a random outbreak of touchy-feeliness. Underpinning the idea is some fundamentally sound Internet business logic. Here's how the authors explain it:

"Technological doors have opened wide to a new global, electronic economy. But the new economy is not built simply on fast distribution of information. This new economy is built upon a central premise of continuous change. In other words, we the people have to *create new information:* ideas that have not been thought of before. Thus the new economy rewards constant improvement and innovation, and these are derived from the minds and imaginations of people. To compete, we have to innovate faster than the next guy – who is trying to do the same thing. And of course, the next guy is no longer just in the office building across the street or across town, but could be anywhere, in any garage or carriage-house, in just about any country in the world ... Two phenomena, the end of long-term employment and the growing need for innovation and imagination, have now met, perhaps more accurately, they have clashed. Innovation requires people's passion to contribute; this passion is fed by a certain loyalty to a compelling cause or purpose that will be advanced by your ideas. This, at a time when loyalty to a company is judged to be a thing of the past."

The book unfolds in four key sections. The first, "Culture at the Core," argues that corporate culture is the key driver of growth. The authors describe how a passionate culture is created on purpose, drawing on the vision and values of the company. They explore ways to improve and sustain a meaningful culture through the use of "cultural sustainers" such as story, image, and ritual. Finally in this section they explore how diversity can be harnessed to play a positive role.

The book's second section, "Leadership Practices: Inspiring Passion-Driven Growth," deals with the leadership style required in passion-driven cultures to sustain and build on what is already there. The qualities of personal integrity and open communication are vital leadership skills, as is the ability of a leader to act as a role model for others. this section also explores how the right kind of leadership can inspire the "breakthrough thinking" needed to thrive.

The third section, "Management Practices," explores how the right use of core business tools and skills, including measurement, marketing, and customer relations, can generate success for the passion-driven company.

The final section brings together eight business and academic players, including Steve Ballmer (President, Microsoft Corporation), HP's Lew Platt and the Chairman and CEO of Novell Eric Schmidt, to participate in a "dialogue on the future" with particular emphasis on electronic commerce. Their broad conclusion? That, as Moore expresses it, "Technology itself interests us, but it's what technology can help us to do for others that inspires us ... Without the technology, these tasks would be harder, but without the passion of caring people, these tasks simply wouldn't get done."

*Clicks and Mortar* proves that passion plus technology is an equation that demonstrably can work. The fact that the authors employed these principles and ideas during their involvement in the meteoric rise of the Charles Schwab Corporation is a clear indication that their ideas have value. The authors write unambiguously that "this book is about organizational transformation": the use of that phrase alone makes this book unusual compared to others featured. What is most striking though is Pottruck and Moore's absolute faith that, in any business endeavor – be it clicks or bricks – the difference that makes the difference is the centrality of the human heart.

### Does building culture waste precious time?

"With results measured quarter to quarter and competitive pressures demanding ever-faster decisions, any practice that sounds like it will slow things down feels antithetical to business success. Any principle that requires an attention to process, such as culture building, can seem useless. Building and reinforcing culture takes time, lots of it, and it can seem like a waste or a luxury in a world with a premium on speed.

"But ignoring cultural construction breeds discontent and actually slows progress. Investing time in alignment is like tuning an engine; it creates efficiency that will not only pay off in results, it will make the whole journey smoother and more fulfilling."

Taken from *Clicks and Mortar*

## *The authors*

David S. Pottruck is President and co-CEO of the Charles Schwab Corporation. Terry Pearce is President of Leadership Communication, and an executive communications officer at Schwab. He also teaches at the Haas School of Business at the University of California, Berkeley.

## *Sources and further reading*

Pottruck, David S, and Pearce, Terry (2000) *Clicks and Mortar: Passion Driven Growth in an Internet Driven World*, Jossey Bass, USA.
There is a companion Website located at:
www.josseybass.com/clicksandmortar.shtml

Schein, Edgar H (1992) *Organizational Culture and Leadership*, Jossey-Bass, USA.
Highly recommended for those who want to take their exploration of organizational culture further.

# JONAS RIDDERSTRÅLE AND KJELL NORDSTRÖM

## *Funky Business*

## 2000

O n the face of it, a business book by two Swedish professors about how successful companies differ from their competitors doesn't sound like the most riveting of reads. But *Funky Business* is no dry theoretical tome; and authors Ridderstråle and Nordström are not your standard-issue academics. Unless, that is, it's normal for Swedish business professors to shave their heads, wear leather trousers, describe themselves as funksters, and call their public appearances gigs rather than seminars.

Perhaps it *now* sounds like you are in for a trip through some familiar corners of the new economy in a light-weight and gimmicky manner redolent of Tom Peters at his worst i.e. paddling at the shallow end. Far from it. This book draws extensively from rigorously researched data but presents its findings with wit and intelligence reinforced with excellent examples.

Ridderstråle and Nordström are convinced that we are moving towards a state of super capitalism, with near friction-free markets. As a result, every supplier everywhere has access to the same resources, ideas, methods and technology. The catch is that every consumer now has access to fantastic choice.

In such a world, they say that time and talent are the two critical commodities and it is how companies deal with these two factors that determines which companies fall by the wayside and which move through to the next round. The goal, and this is as good as it gets, is to be, as the authors put it, "momentarily ahead of the game."

The authors offer a theoretical model for achieving this fleeting competitive advantage in the form of Funky Inc., a company that is flat, open, and small. It's a company in which, to take only a few samples from the *Funky Business* smorgasbord, you would:

- Signal what you stand for in terms of values (i.e. branding) and then taking them with you on a trip of relentless innovation and change.
- Recognize that being average is not good enough: the goal is to be 100% completely right for a specific market, not ordinary and 95% right to everybody.
- Change the frame of reference from what you are selling to what the customer is actually buying – the two are not always the same! Get on the same "vibe" as your customer.
- Take risks, accept even welcome failure, and spurn all things average.
- Offer products and services that constantly take the customer by surprise. For example, on-line bookseller bol.com's "Free copy for a friend" week which ran in June 2000 increased sales three-fold with a campaign that emphasized giving a present rather than receiving a freebie. Claimed as a global first, when a customer bought a CD or book from the top 40, they could nominate a friend who was sent a copy at no charge.
- Bring your products to market faster than anybody else, and replace them frequently. Most of Hewlett-Packard's revenues, for example, derive from products that are less than a year old.
- Use your core competencies to enter new industries without hesitation.

It is not easy to characterize *Funky Business*. The book overflows with provocative ideas, but it is not a practical "how to survive the future" road map; nor is it a set of predictions on "what the future will be like." It is a comprehensive and coherent philosophy – the philosophy of FUNK. Unusually, in an age of instant gurus and ready prescriptions, Ridderstråle and Nordström leave it unambiguously up to the reader to embrace, integrate and apply the thinking contained in the book.

## *The* Funky Business *guide to leadership and management*

"Leadership and management are more important than ever before. Gurus and commentators have been proclaiming this for years, maybe because it justified their existence. Now it is reality.

"This is the age of time and talent, where we are selling, exploiting, organizing, hiring and packaging time and talent. The most critical resource wears shoes and walks out the door around five o'clock every day. As a result, management and leadership are keys to competitive advantage. They differentiate you from the mass. How you attract, retain and motivate your people is more important than technology; how you treat your customers and suppliers, more important than technology. How a company is managed and how a company is led are vital differentiators. They can create sustainable uniqueness. But at the same time as management and leadership have reached maturity as potent competitive weapons, their very nature has changed.

"The boss is dead. No longer can we believe in a leader who claims to know more about everything and who is always right. Management by numbers is history. Management by fear won't work. If management is people, management must become humanagement.

"The job is dead. No longer can we believe in having a piece of paper saying job description at the top. The new realities call for far greater flexibility. Throughout most of the twentieth century, managers averaged one job and one career. Now, we are talking about two careers and seven jobs. The days of the long-serving corporate man, safe and sound in the dusty recesses of the corporation, are long gone. Soon the emphasis will be on getting a life instead of a career, and work will be viewed as a series of gigs or projects.

"Inevitably, new roles demand new skills. Thirty years ago, we had to learn one new skill per year. Now, it is one new skill per day. Tomorrow, it may be one new skill per hour. Skills like networking – in 1960, the average manager had to learn 25 names throughout their entire career; today we must learn 25 new names every single month. Tomorrow, it may be 25 new names per week."

Taken from *Funky Business*

## The authors

Jonas Ridderstråle is based at the Institute of International Business at the Stockholm School of Economics. He is on the board of directors of Stokke Fabrikker, Swedish Internet company Spary Ventures and the US digital change agent Razorfish.

Kjell Nordström is based at the Center for Advanced Studies in Leadership at the Stockholm School of Economics. In his spare time he is an art collector He holds an MBA and a doctorate.

## Sources and further reading

Ridderstråle, Jonas, and Nordström, Kjell (2000) *Funky Business*, ft.com.
You can visit the funksters at www.funkybusiness.com

# JONATHAN ROSENOER, DOUGLAS ARMSTRONG & J. RUSSELL GATES

## The Clickable Corporation

## 1999

*T*he *Clickable Corporation* has a subtitle – *Successful Strategies for Capturing the Internet Advantage* – that makes its intentions very clear. Based on research by three consultants at global consultancy Arthur Andersen, and drawing on evidence from 25 companies including Barnes & Noble, Federal Express, Amazon, and Dell, this book sets out to offer an accessible guide aimed at business people who are looking to make optimal and profitable use of the Web.

Rosenoer, Armstrong and Gates, displaying a level of certainty that seemingly only management consultants can ever muster, tell us that there are eight value propositions that a company must offer through its Website – knowledge, choice, convenience, customization, savings, community, entertainment, and trust. To look at each in turn:

1   *Knowledge.* Customers can retrieve information about products and services that was previously inaccessible or available only at some cost and trouble.
2   *Choice.* A well-designed Website helps customers to sift through the choices available and make an optimal decision.
3   *Convenience.* Because the Internet removes barriers of time and space, customers can act when it suits them and deal with providers from anywhere in the world.
4   *Customization.* As Amazon have shown, offering customers personalized attention and the opportunity to shape the Website's service to their specific needs yields dividends.
5   *Savings.* The Internet can be used to streamline processes, eliminate barriers, and give better control of the supply chain. In this way, costs can be reduced and consequent savings passed on to customers.

6    *Community.* Creating online communities and focusing on their
     interests and needs, provides an opportunity to offer products and
     services to an audience that is already predisposed to the offering.
7    *Entertainment.* The Internet's capacity for providing fun experiences
     and interactivity can leverage customer attraction.
8    *Trust.* It is vital to dispel customer doubts by offering high levels
     of service and security.

For each of the eight factors, the authors give examples drawn from the
practical experience of the 25 companies studied. They then go on to
suggest a process that a company would need to go through to assess
its readiness for on-line trading, and outline the skills needed to set up
and run a successful Website.

In *The Clickable Corporation*, the authors provide an informative and
accessible guide to the merits and challenges of setting up an Internet
business. However, anybody already steeped in Internet thinking may
find the book lacks depth. Also, the case study approach used by the
authors means that the contents are liable to date quickly. So, despite
its great name and its current relevance, it would be a surprise if *The
Clickable Corporation* reappears in *Writing the New Economy's* second
edition.

## Reality check: six misconceptions about Internet business

### Nobody makes money on the Web

The media's frequent stories about the Internet's profitless companies
typically overlook the fact that many currently spend more than they
earn, because they are building infrastructures from scratch. Wall Street
understands: many Internet start-ups boast stock-market valuations
in significant multiples of their revenues, giving them easy access to
the capital they need to grow.

### It doesn't hurt to wait and see

Many companies prefer to let others in their industry break the
trail and cope with the headaches that Internet leaders sometimes
encounter. That strategy didn't benefit Barnes & Noble, Inc. It simply
watched an Internet-only bookseller, Amazon.com, Inc., seize a strong
first-mover advantage (and a market capitalization that tops Borders

Group, Inc., and Barnes & Noble combined). Now Barnes & Noble is catching up, but not without paying a price.

## A "Doing business on the Web" costs too much

It certainly isn't cheap, but many companies say the benefits far outweigh the costs. Cisco Systems, Inc., which attributes $500 million savings in annual operating expenses to its networked business model, reports that online sales have resulted in about a 15% increase in account executive and sales engineer productivity. The benefits for Cisco have even spread to the recruiting process, where receiving resumes via the Internet has led to an $8 million recruiting cost reduction.

## Internet customers are vulnerable to theft

Some holdouts fear losing customers, who worry that Internet intruders will steal their credit card data. If this were an uncontrollable problem – which it isn't – scores of the nation's biggest companies would not be conducting millions of credit card transactions, safely and smoothly, round the clock, every day of the week.

## Websites are vulnerable to competitors

The perceived fear here is that your site may be picked clean by competitors poaching proprietary information about your customers, products, or services. This isn't the case. Actually, some Internet companies rather hope their competitors do snoop around their Websites. Autobytel.com and Coldwell Banker Real Estate Corporation, for example, believe that it makes good business sense to let competitors see what you have for sale.

## The Internet isn't big enough

More than 100 million people are already online. At the current growth rate, that number will reach one billion within five years – an order of acceleration and connectivity never seen before. And even in five years, the vast majority of the world's people won't yet have owned computers, much less have gone online, ensuring future Internet growth for years to come. If that isn't a mass market, what is?

Derived from *The Clickable Corporation*

## The authors

Jonathan Rosenoer is Director, Electronic Commerce Readiness, in the computer risk management practice at Arthur Andersen. He has spent the past 10 years developing commercial online systems and looking at associated business risk and process issues. He is the author of *Cyberlaw: the Law of the Internet.*

Douglas Armstrong is Director, Marketing and Digital Communications, for Arthur Andersen Knowledge Enterprises. He directs marketing and business development activities for the Virtual Learning Network™ and Knowledgespace™, Arthur Andersen's award-winning electronic knowledge services. Armstrong also leads Web design and development for the firm's Internet sites.

J. Russell Gates is a partner in the Chicago Office of Arthur Andersen. He leads their computer risk management practice in North America and is the world-wide head of Arthur Andersen's Electronic Commerce Risk Consulting and Assurance initiatives.

## Sources and further reading

Rosenoer, Jonathan, Armstrong, Douglas and Gates, J. Russell (1999) *The Clickable Corporation*, Free Press, USA.
The book has a companion Website that can be found at: www.arthurandersen.com/clickable

EVAN SCHWARTZ

*Digital Darwinism*

1999

Y   ou, I and Shakespeare know that all that glisters is not gold.
    Nonetheless, a book title that grings together two of the big-
    gest managerial buzzwords of recent times exerts a certain
    fascination. So what is *Digital Darwinism*? According to Evan
Schwartz in an interview published on Amazon.com, it is "a different
way of looking at the Web economy and how it's co-evolving with the
larger business world around it. It's a way of looking at the Web as
an ecosystem, where the players are scrounging for money and are
competing and co-operating with each other as if they were a species
in a natural environment"

This is a fascinating premise and one which merits rather more
depth than Schwartz brings to the topic. There is a 17-page introduction
called "Frenetic Evolution" in which he notes some interesting parallels
between Darwin's theory of evolution and the on-line world. But he goes
no further in substantive terms. There are a few links made to what lies
at the heart of *Digital Darwinism*, namely "seven breakthrough strategies
for surviving in the cut-throat Web economy," but occasional allusions to
"survival guides" don't constitute the grand theory that Schwartz seems
to promise at the outset. The irony is that the seven strategies themselves
are a neat encapsulation of what a business – be it an Internet start-up or
a bricks-and-mortar offshoot – should be doing to achieve Web success.

The seven strategies are as follows:

1   *Build a brand that stands for solving problems.* Selling products cheaply
    over the Web doesn't in itself guarantee survival – you need to
    identify a specific set of issues faced by customers and then go on to
    put in place a set of interactive services that address those problems.
    In this way, you create a "solution brand," a unique, comprehensive
    solution that is resilient against aggressive competition.

2    *Allow your prices to fluctuate freely with supply and demand.* Online auction houses like eBay are bringing dynamic pricing to the masses; shopbots are roaming the net seeking out the best deal on any given item and feeding that information to your current or potential customers; when products and services are nearing the end of the most productive part of their life cycle, your only choice is between dropping your price or holding excess inventory; and don't forget that surges in demand at times like Christmas may enable you to charge a premium.

3    *Let affiliate partners do your marketing for you.* Recruit affiliate partners to sell your products and thus spread your marketing messages to the far reaches of cyberspace; as competing affiliate networks increase, boost your commissions to your most successful partners; take advantage of "viral marketing," the Internet's ability to spread ideas and information quickly and cheaply.

4    *Create valuable bundles of information and services.* Subscribers who pay money for your information service have a financial incentive to return to your site regularly; bundled up information generates a better financial return than selling items singly; concentrate on a specific information niche – the more generalist your service, the more likely that it will be available somewhere else at no cost.

5    *Sell custom-made products online, then manufacture them.* The economics of sell and build are inherently superior to build and sell, as Dell Computers demonstrate.

6    *Add new value to transactions between buyers and sellers.* Intermediaries are under some threat from the Web but there are ways they can add value, e.g. develop a neutral meeting space where buyers and sellers can find each and place/receive orders efficiently; alternatively, form an affiliate relationship with a cybermediary to generate leads on your behalf.

7    *Integrate digital commerce with absolutely everything.* Set up effective feedback loops between different business channels to share best practice and to enable cross-promotional initiatives; ensure that your Website supports new technologies like palm-tops, digital phones, car computers and so on.

Through his seven strategies, Schwartz provides the reader with a sophisticated and convincing set of tools to help create, expand or enhance an on-line business. He deploys some highly relevant case studies to support his line of argument. The book's only weakness is that its title – which is probably in a two-horse race with *Clicking the*

*Corporation* for being the most eye- and imagination-grabbing of all the 50 books reviewed – doesn't really reflect its contents.

## Evan Schwartz on frenetic evolution

"When Charles Darwin presented his theory of evolution in 1859, he described a world in which only the fittest survive, a world in which species must constantly adapt to their changing environment or face extinction, a world in which organisms must continue to grow in a profitable direction and develop new skills and traits or perish, a world in which life-forms must look around and learn with whom to co-operate and with whom to compete, a world in which the surrounding conditions for life can, suddenly and drastically, improve or take a turn for the worse. Darwin even wrote that we are all 'bound together in a complex web of relations.'

"This lexicon applies unmistakably to the digital business land-scape now flourishing and mutating across the World Wide Web. 'Many more individuals of each species are born than can possibly survive,' Darwin wrote. 'Consequently, there is a frequently recurring struggle for existence, and it follows that any being, if it varies however slightly in any manner profitable to itself under the complex conditions of life, will have a better chance of surviving, and thus be naturally selected.' And just as Darwin observed that competition for food and resources leads to principles of natural evolution, we can see that brutal market forces in the increasingly cut-throat Web economy lead to new strategies for economic survival.

"Indeed, the Web is in the throes of an especially frenetic evolution. As an environment that can sustain economic life, the Web has given birth to entirely new species of start-ups and enterprises that could not have existed previously. These new economic organisms are, in turn, forcing older corporate species to evolve in new ways, producing new business models and characteristics necessary for their own survival.

"Still, evolution takes time to manifest itself in a significant way. In the natural world, often it takes thousands of years for major or even slight changes to become apparent. The Web may be a universe of digital information in which companies can change their appearance and switch their survival plans in a matter of weeks, but evolution writ large still requires a more significant time frame to produce outcomes, results, effects, and lessons learned the hard way."

Taken from *Digital Darwinism*

### Reality check: UK dot.com cash "running out"

In May 2000, PwC, the professional services firm, issued a report warning that most UK-floated Internet companies could run out of cash within 15 months because of high marketing and expansion costs.

PwC claimed that 25 out of 28 listed companies could burn through their cash pile by August 2001 – well short of most projected break-even points – if they continued to spend at the current rate. One in four companies has less than six months' worth of cash left.

Marketing and technology, which can account for 50 per cent or more of the cost of goods at dot.coms, are being blamed for eating into cash reserves at Web companies that do not yet earn anything like enough revenue to cover these costs.

This report, coming in the same month as the high-profile demise of boo.com, triggered a real crisis of confidence in dot.com businesses, which up to that point seemed to be re-writing the traditional laws of business. Profit soon, rather than profit eventually, has become the order of the day.

## *The author*

A former editor at *Business Week*, Evan I. Schwartz is a regular contributor to the *New York Times* and *Wired* magazine. His previous book, *Webonomics,* was a finalist for both the *Financial Times* Global Business Book Award and the Computer Press Award. He now lives in Brookline, Massachusetts

## *Sources and further reading*

Schwartz, Evan I. (1999) *Digital Darwinism: Seven Breakthrough Business Strategies for Surviving in the Cut-throat Web Economy,* Broadway Books, USA.
The book has a companion Website which is located at:
www.digitaldarwinism.com

Schwartz, Evan I. (1997) *Webonomics,* Broadway Books, USA.
Webonomics is "the study of the production, distribution and consumption of goods, services and ideas over the World Wide Web." Schwartz

defines nine essential principles for growing a business on the Web, using case studies to document some successes and failures.

Kelly, Kevin (1994) *Out of Control,* Addison Wesley, USA.
Anybody interested in exploring the metaphor of the Internet as eco-system might well find value in exploring this book in which Kelly identifies nine laws to account for the organizing principles that can be found operating in natural systems. The full text can also be found at http://well.com/user/kk/OutOfControl/

# CARL SHAPIRO & HAL R. VARION

## *Information Rules*

## 1998

"Annual income twenty pounds, annual expenditure nineteen nineteen six, result happiness. Annual income twenty pounds, annual expenditure twenty pounds ought and six, result misery"

M r Micawber's model of economic prudence, that being in profit mattered, has long since been banished to the realms of Dickensian quaintness. "How unsophisticated," said the credit card generation. "How unnecessary," commented the Internet startups.

New century: new economy; new economics. When lastminute.com's flotation early in 2000 gave them the same market value as venerable bricks-and-mortar retailer WH Smith, it did seem to confirm that the economic paradigm had been shifted by the upstart online businesses. Don't worry about this year's numbers, just imagine the potential a few years down the road. Share prices soared.

Then the markets tumbled, and a series of high-profile dot.com humiliations confirmed that the Internet's period of grace is over. So what is the lesson from all this?

The easy answer is that profits still matter. A broader message comes from the authors of *Information Rules*, Carl Shapiro and Hal R. Varian: Ignore basic economic principles at your own risk. Technology changes. Economic laws do not.

Their book, highly rated by Kevin Kelly among others, sets out to show that classic economic principles can still offer strategic value in a marketplace that depends on cutting-edge information technology.

The result is a book that is rigorous with its analysis, convincing in its grip of the subject (the authors are both bona fide economists), and oozing gravitas.

That said, Shapiro and Varian do lighten the load for the reader by including plenty of real-life examples.

Among the issues they explore are: pricing and versioning information; rights management; recognizing and managing lock-in; switching costs; and how to factor government policy and regulation into strategy. They conclude each section with a set of lessons derived from their analysis. For example, they offer the following pieces of advice on the matter of pricing information:

- Analyze and understand how much you invest in producing and selling your product.
- If you are forced to compete in a commodity market, be aggressive but not greedy.
- Differentiate your product by personalizing the information and the price.
- Invest in collecting and analyzing data about you market.
- Use the information about your customers to sell them personalized products at personalized prices.
- Analyze the profitability of selling to groups, e.g. site licenses

These pointers might seem a little glib on their own but, unlike some other texts, their advice is merely a top-cut of findings that are substantiated elsewhere in the book.

*Information Rules* is not by any means an easy read but it is accessible to the general reader who is prepared to concentrate a bit. Highly recommended for chastened dot.com businesses.

### Reality check: Shapiro and Varian – what distinguishes their approach from others?

"First, this book is not about trends. Lots of books about the impact of technology are attempts to forecast the future. You've heard that work will become more decentralized, more organic, and more flexible. You've heard about flat organizations and unlimited bandwidth. But the methodology for forecasting these trends is unclear; typically, it is just extrapolation from recent developments. Our forecasting, such as it is, is based on durable economic principles that have been proven to work in practice.

"Second, this book is not about *vocabulary*. We're not going to invent any new buzzwords (although we do hope to resurrect a few old ones). Our goal is to introduce new terms only when they actually describe a useful concept; there will be no vocabulary for the sake of vocabulary. We won't talk about 'cyberspace,' the 'cybereconomy,' or cyber-anything.

"Third, this book is not about *analogies*. We won't tell you that devising business strategy is like restoring an ecosystem, fighting a war, or making love. Business strategy is business strategy and though analogies can sometimes be helpful, they can also be misleading. Our view is that analogies can be an effective way to *communicate* strategies, but they are a very dangerous way to analyze strategies.

"We seek models, not trends; concepts, not vocabulary; and analysis, not analogies. We firmly believe the models, the concepts, and the analysis will provide you with a deeper understanding of the fundamental forces at work in today's high-tech industries and enable you to craft winning strategies for tomorrow's network economy."

Taken from *Information Rules*

## The authors

Carl Shapiro is the Transamerica Professor of Business Strategy, Haas School of Business and Department of Economics, University of California at Berkeley. During 1995/96, he served as Deputy Assistant Attorney General for Economics, in the Antitrust Division of the US Department of Justice.

Hal R. Varian is the Class of 1944 Professor and the Dean of the School of Information Management and Systems, with joint appointments at the Haas School of Business and the Department of Economics, University of California at Berkeley.

## Sources and further reading

Shapiro, Carl, and Varian, Hal R. (1999) *Information Rules: a Strategic Guide to the Network Economy*, Harvard Business School Press, USA.

Co-author Hal Varian oversees a Website called *The Information Economy*, which lists hundreds of papers, works in progress, and links to other new economy Websites. An almost overwhelming resource but one that hasn't been bettered.

http://www.sims.berkeley.edu/resources/infoecon/

# DAVID SIEGEL

## *Futurize your Enterprise*

### 1999

"E veryone understands that the Internet is changing business," says Siegel in *Futurize your Enterprise*, "but most companies still don't understand how to approach the Web. They've applied new kinds of marketing and technology, they've put their catalogues online, they put 'com' at the end of their names, and they have little to show for their efforts. that's because the limiting factor online isn't technology, branding, or bandwidth – it's mindset."

According to Siegel, many companies fail to truly understand how e-commerce works, and as a result they fall into some or all of what he calls "the six common traps of e-commerce," namely:

1   *Not taking the medium seriously:* e.g. companies treat the Web like a trade show or simply an extension of its paper catalogues, or simply copy their competitors. It almost seems more important to look like they know what they're doing than actually to know.

2   *Trying to please everyone:* e.g. packing the Website with so many features that the customer is baffled. In trying to please everybody, the Website satisfies nobody.

3   *Focusing on technology, rather than people:* you can tell how far your company has fallen into the technology trap by how long it takes to make a change on the site. If it's easy to make changes to the home page, that's a good sign. If it takes seven days to correct a spelling error, the technology is more of a barrier than an aid.

4   *Focusing on brands and messages:* e.g. when companies go down this route, all too often the site is over-controlled and carries too much bland content. Customer comments are discouraged in case they are critical – the site is run by spin doctors.

5   *The introverted Website:* i.e. the site is organized around internal issues rather than needs of customers.
6   *Taking themselves too seriously:* i.e. being so intent in putting in place the content that the company believes the customer ought to want to know about that (1) the site seems pompous and humorless, and (2) the real interests of customers are never know because nobody asks the question.

*Futurize your Enterprise* is really about how companies can avoid these traps and, more positively, become a meaningful player in what Siegel calls the Customer-Led Revolution that will connect almost two billion people to the Web by the year 2010. The book is organized in four parts.

In Part I, Siegel shows how companies like Microsoft and Dell have reorganized around customer groups – rather than around product, content, or service offerings – and this structure allows those companies to listen and respond to customer needs faster. "In the next five years," he writes, "those who understand the Internet will reorganize around their most profitable customer groups and change their companies from the outside in. Microsoft recently made this transition. I believe most companies will learn from their experience and follow suit."

Siegel concludes this part by defining the Truth Economy, in which honest, open companies prosper while companies with something to hide are ignored or attacked.

In Part II of the book, he outlines the six meetings that he believes are necessary to build a proper support system for a customer-led Website. The meetings revolve around gaining internal commitment, customer segmentation, actively listening to customers, developing appropriate measures, customer modeling, and mapping out a strategy for implementation.

In the third part, probably the most useful part of the book, Siegel takes us through 8 fictitious case studies, covering various prototype businesses like a book superstore, a grocery store, a drug manufacturer. The case studies demonstrate clearly how properly aligned, customer-led companies use the Internet to benefit employees and customers equally. The keys to success seem to revolve around on-going dialogue with customers, having employees who are empowered to respond to new demands, and putting in place processes that enable on-line businesses to follow customer behavior and needs closely.

In the final section, Siegel offers some predictions about how the business landscape might develop over the next 10 years, as most of the world goes online. He does this by creating a number of Internet user

> ## Zeitbite
>
> "The first printed books imitated handwritten manuscripts. The first photographs were portraits. Many early motion pictures captured theatrical plays on screen. So it's not surprising that in the late 1990s, companies tried hard to re-create their familiar business environments online. They thought the World Wide Web would provide the new 'front-end' to their existing business practices. Re-creating the physical world online is a temporary, transitional and often unnecessary strategy."
>
> Taken from *Futurize your Enterprise*

categories such as The Job Seeker, The Student, The Homemaker, and The Lawyer and then speculating about how the Internet might evolve for people in these categories.

*Futurize your Enterprise* is packed with insights and provocative assertions about the future shape of the Internet. The book is a real wake-up call for companies who think that the Internet is just starting to settle into recognizable business patterns, and that their on-line presence can be run using the same management mindset that runs the bricks-and-mortar business.

### Dell – a model e-business

"Dell Computer Corporation is one of the computer industry's most progressive companies. Michael Dell built an e-business before anyone coined the term. Dell knew his customers. He gave them a way around the usual routes to procurement. He let them order computers one at a time, while still giving them the contract discount. He let them order by phone, with a credit card, even on weekends. Rather than building new products in long planning cycles and having the products sit on the shelf, he started building customers' products as soon as they ordered them.

"When the Web came along, Dell.com was a natural extension of the offline business. It's impossible to tell the company from its Website. The site is simply another aspect of doing business with Dell. The entire site is aligned by customer categories, not hardware model lines. The site directs each type of customer to a special second-level page, where the entire line of Dell products is presented and explained in a way that is relevant to each customer's needs.

"Dell truly partners with its business customers online. More then 15,000 customers now have Premier Pages – an extranet that ties Dell's order-entry system right into the customer's procurement software to make ordering and tracking easy.

"Dell brings customers into the product-planning and manufacturing processes, not just the sales process, and management encourages everyone in the company to have contact with customers. That broad employee–customer interface prevents the communication bottleneck that occurs if only the Web team is in touch with e-customers.

"These employee–customer relationships not only foster loyalty to Dell but will help the company adapt in the future."

Taken from *Futurize your Enterprise*

## The author

David Siegel is Chairman of Studio Verso, a Web-design and strategy company, and President of Siegel Vision, an e-strategy company. His clients include Hewlett-Packard, Lucent, Sony, and NASA. He serves as advisor to the HTML and STYLE committees of the W3C, a consortium in charge of further development of standards on the Web. Previous books include *Creating Killer Web Sites* and *Secrets of Successful Web Sites*.

## Sources and further reading

Siegel, David (1999) *Futurize your Enterprise: Business Strategy in the Age of the e-Customer*, John Wiley, USA.
*Futurize your Enterprise* comes in seven parts. Four of them are in the book, and the other three are online at www.Futurizenow.com. The Website has an online boot camp for executives, updated links, and ongoing discussions. Worth investigating.

Siegel features in the March/April 2000 issue of the *Harvard Business Review* as the lead responder for that issue's case study.

# THOMAS STEWART
## *Intellectual Capital*
### 1997

 emember the time when capital could be viewed in purely financial or physical terms? It showed up in the buildings and equipment owned, it could be found in the corporate balance sheets. In recent years, though, we've all had to get to grips with an altogether more elusive, intangible form of asset: intellectual capital.

*Intellectual Capital* by Thomas Stewart has proved itself in the marketplace as the definitive guide to understanding and managing intangible assets. In it, the author provides a framework for, practical guide to, and theory of the significance of intellectual capital (defined by Stewart as "packaged useful knowledge").

Intellectual capital can be broken down into three areas:

*   *Human capital:* the knowledge that resides within the heads of employees that is relevant to the purpose of the organization. Human capital is formed and deployed, writes Stewart, "when more of the time and talent of the people who work in a company is devoted to activities that result in innovation." Human capital can grow in two ways: "when the organization uses more of what people know, and when people know more stuff that is useful to the organization." Unleashing the human capital resident in the organization requires "minimizing mindless tasks, meaningless paperwork, unproductive infighting."

    However, human capital, as well as being needed by the organization, also has a value for the individual worker. In 1994, Peter Drucker wrote that "the true investment in the knowledge society is not in machines and tools but in the knowledge of the knowledge worker ... The industrial worker needed the capitalist infinitely more than the capitalist needed the industrial worker ... In the knowledge society the most probable assumption for organizations – and certainly the assumption on which they have to conduct their affairs – is that they need knowledge workers far more than knowledge workers need them."

- *Customer capital:* the value of a company's ongoing relationships with the people or organizations to which it sells. Indicators of customer capital include market share, customer retention and defection rates, and profit per customer. Stewart's belief is that "customer capital is probably – and startlingly when you think about it – the worst managed of all intangible assets. Many businesses don't even know who their customers are."
- *Structural capital:* the knowledge retained within the organization that becomes company property. Stewart calls this "knowledge that doesn't go home at night." Structural capital "belongs to the organization as a whole. It can be reproduced and shared." Examples of structural capital include technologies, inventions, publications, and business processes.

Understanding what intellectual capital amounts to is only part of the story for organizations. The real value comes in being able to capture and deploy it. To this end, Stewart offers the following ten principles for managing intellectual capital:

1 Companies don't own human and customer capital. Only by recognizing the shared nature of these assets can a company manage and profit from these assets.
2 To create human capital it can use, a company needs to foster teamwork, communities of practice, and other social forms of learning.
3 Organizational wealth is created around skills and talents that are proprietary and scarce. To manage and develop human capital companies must recognize unsentimentally that people with these talents are assets to invest in. Others are costs to be minimized.
4 Structural assets (those intangible assets the company owns) are the easiest to manage but those that customers care least about.
5 Move from amassing knowledge just-in-case to having information that customers need ready-to-hand, and that which they *might* need within reasonable reach.
6 Information and knowledge can and should substitute for expensive physical and financial assets.
7 Knowledge work is custom work.

## Zeitbite

"If the subject of intellectual capital ever spawns a business fad, it will be under the guise of 'knowledge management,' because there's money to be made selling software, systems, and consulting services with the touted goal of allowing every person in an organization to be able to lay his hands on the collected wisdom of all his colleagues."

How prophetic Thomas Stewart's words turned out to be. Within six months of the publication of *Intellectual Capital*, knowledge management had indeed become the latest business fad.

8   Every company should re-analyze the value chain of the industry that it participates in to see what information is most crucial.
9   Focus on the flow of information not the flow of materials.
10  Human, structural and customer capital work together. It is not enough to invest in people, systems and customer separately. They can support each other or detract from each other.

Since *Intellectual Capital* first appeared, there have been a flood of books on knowledge management hitting the marketplace. In an age of lightweight books on the new information age, this book is a heavyweight, which explains not only why intellectual capital will be the foundation of corporate success in the new century, but which also offers practical guidance to companies about how to make best use of their intangible assets.

## Reality check

Tucked away in *Intellectual Capital* is a chapter called "Your career in the Information Age" which contains more wisdom and insight in 18 pages than a shelf-load of traditional career management texts.

In it, Stewart makes six observations about careers in the 21st century:

1   A career is a series of gigs, not a series of steps.
2   Project management is the furnace in which successful careers are made.

**Zeitbite**

Knowledge assets, like money or equipment, exist and are worth cultivating only in the context of strategy. You cannot define and manage intellectual assets unless you know what you want to do with them.

Thomas Stewart, *Intellectual Capital*

3    In the new organization, power flows from expertise, not from position.
4    Most roles in an organization can be performed by either insiders or outsiders.
5    Careers are made in markets not hierarchies.
6    The fundamental career choice is not between one company and another, but between specializing and generalizing.

Implicit in these observations is a challenge to anybody currently working in an organization. We all know that there are no jobs for life in a general sense. But what about *our* job, *our* life? Below are 10 questions that are designed to be a career wake-up call. If a number of these click, you need to act:

1    Have you learned anything new in the last six months?
2    Is your job easy?
3    Could somebody do your job for less?
4    If your job were open, would you get it?
5    Are you being milked by being kept in the same role?
6    Do you know what you contribute?
7    What specific skills could you take to the marketplace?
8    What would you do if your job disappeared tomorrow? Next year?
9    Is your heart in it?
10   Are you worried about your job? (If you aren't, you probably should be.)

Derived from *Intellectual Capital* by Thomas Stewart

## *The author*

Thomas A. Stewart is a member of the board of editors of *Fortune* magazine. He pioneered the field of intellectual capital in a series of articles that earned him an international reputation, the Planning Forum calling him "the leading proponent of knowledge management in the business press." He lives in Manhattan.

## *Sources and further reading*

Stewart, Thomas A. (1997) *Intellectual Capital: The New Wealth of Organizations*, Doubleday, USA.

Edvinsson, Leif, and Malone, Michael (1997) *Intellectual Capital*, HarperBusiness, USA.

Drucker, Peter F. (1994) "The age of social transformation," *The Atlantic Monthly*, November.

# DON TAPSCOTT, DAVID TICOLL & ALEX LOWY

## Digital Capital

## 2000

W hen we compiled the list of books to feature in *Writing the New Economy*, one of our easiest decisions was to include "the latest Tapscott."

The phrase is significant. Many business writers seem content to produce one decent book with some worthwhile ideas, but they then rehash and repackage the material in subsequent books – the law of diminishing authorial returns. Tapscott is different: with each new book he goes deeper into the heart of the new economy.

*Digital Capital*, co-written with two colleagues, explores how the net and digital media open up new ways to create wealth. It features companies like Shwab, eBay, Cisco, MP3 and Linux that have transformed the rules of competition in their industries by making revolutionary offerings to their customers. They did not achieve this alone: combining with like-minded partners with complementary skills was the key.

Tapscott, Ticoll and Lowy call these Internet-based partnerships or alliances "business webs," or "b-webs" for short. A b-web, according to the authors, is "a distinct system of suppliers, distributors, commerce services providers, infrastructure providers and customers that use the Internet for their primary business communications and transactions." Although alliance-based, a b-web typically has an identifiable lead partner that formally orchestrates their strategies and processes.

The core of *Digital Capital* is devoted to describing five distinct types of b-web:

- *Agoras.* The agoras of ancient Greece were centers for public intercourse and commercial transactions. The authors apply the term to "markets where buyers and sellers meet to freely negotiate and assign value to goods." Price discovery mechanisms include one-to-one haggling, multiparty auctions and exchanges. An example of an Agora is eBay, the Internet-based consumer auction Website.

- *Aggregations.* "In an aggregation b-web, one company – like Wal-Mart – leads…, positioning itself as a value-adding intermediary between producers and customers." The lead aggregator selects products and services, targets particular market segments, sets prices and ensures fulfillment. Retailers and wholesalers are examples of aggregations,
- *Value chains.* The lead organization structures a b-web network to produce a highly integrated value proposition. The output satisfies a customer order or market opportunity and the seller has the final say in pricing.
- *Alliances.* "The most ethereal of b-webs," alliances aim for high-value integration without a formal hierarchy of control. Alliances include online communities, research initiatives, and shared experiences. The MP3 phenomenon is an alliance.
- *Distributive networks.* These are the b-webs that, in conjunction with the roads, postal and telephones services, and power grids of the industrial economy, keep the new economy alive and mobile. They don't create or consume their cargo – simply pass it around. Examples include data network operators, the new logistic companies and on-line banks

The authors go on to outline the following six-step process for "weaving a b-web":

1 Describe the current value proposition from the customer's viewpoint, that is, why this systems exists.
2 Disaggregate: consider the contributors and their contributions, strengths, and weaknesses. Compare the parts and capabilities of your business to those in other systems.
3 Envision b-web-enabled value through brainstorming and other creative design techniques. Decide what the new value proposition will be.
4 Reaggregate: define what it will take to deliver the new value proposition, including processes, contributors, contributions, applications and technologies, and other success factors.
5 Prepare a value map: Design a visual map that depicts value exchanges in the b-web.
6 Do the b-web mix: Define a b-web typing strategy that will improve your competitive advantages.

Reading *Digital Wealth* reinforces a sense that Tapscott's understanding deepens with each new book he publishes (with or without collaborators). Where this book differs from the majority is that it goes beyond mere description, beyond eye-catching but slight lists of key points (don't be misled by the precis above – there is substantial analysis and commentary underpinning each point). When it comes to characterizing what is driving change in the economy, there are hundreds of books on the market. *Digital Capital* goes well beyond the simplistic sloganizing to offer genuine insight and, even more important, some guidance on practical steps that can be put in place.

## The new alphabet of marketing

"The A, B, C, D, Es of marketing have replaced the four Ps:

- *"Anyplace, anytime, anyway shopping replaces place.* Companies must design integrated strategies for the marketspace and, if appropriate, the marketplace and marketface. Customers want convenience.
- *"B-web customers drive revenue.* Relationship capital is reflected in a brand. Think of customers as part of your b-web and prospects as candidates for relationships, not as markets for your products.
- *"Communication works, not promotion.* One-way media, like broadcasting, can be part of the marketing mix, but the customer decides whether – and with whom – to engage in a one-, two-, or multi-way communication.
- *"Discovery of price replaces fixed price.* The days when companies unilaterally control prices are nearly over.
- *"Experience replaces product.* Customers pay for experiences, not products. Products must be bundled with enhanced, customized services. The automobile experience replaces the product, as the vehicle becomes a platform for transportation, interactive entertainment, safety) doing business, and having fun."

Taken from Digital Capital

## *The authors*

Don Tapscott is Chairman, David Ticoll is CEO, and Alex Lowy is Managing Director of the Alliance for Converging Technologies, an international research and consulting group that advises corporations and governments worldwide on strategy in the digital economy.

The authors can be contacted on digitalcapital@actnet.com

## Sources and further reading

Tapscott, Don, Ticoll, David and Lowy, Alex (2000) *Digital Capital: Harnessing the Power of Business Webs*, Nicholas Brealey, USA.
The Alliance for Converging Technologies has a Website, which can be found at www.actnet.com

Tapscott, Don (1996) *The Digital Economy: Promise and Peril in the Age of Networked Intelligence*, McGraw-Hill, USA.
Explores some of the emerging dynamics of the new economy. More examples than theory or analysis, but good at picking out business trends.

Tapscott, Don (1998) *Growing up Digital: the Rise of the Net Generation*, McGraw-Hill, USA.
Explains how, as it grows up, the net generation is learning to communicate, work, shop, and play in new ways by using the Internet as a basic resource. It is aimed at businessmen, parents, and teachers, giving them some pointers about how to plan for the future.

# ALVIN TOFFLER
## *The Third Wave*
### 1980

T he "Third Wave" referred to in the title of Alvin Toffler's classic is the age of "the super-industrial society" in which the new technologies redefine how people operate at a societal, organizational and personal level. Following two preceding waves (the agricultural phase of civilization's development, followed by the "Second Wave" of industrialization), the Third Wave, Toffler anticipated, would bring with it much anxiety and trauma. It would be characterized by great uncertainty. "Old ways of thinking," he writes, "old formulas, dogmas, and ideologies, no matter how cherished or how useful in the past, no longer fit the facts." He went on: "The world that is fast emerging from the clash of new values and technologies, new geopolitical relationships, new lifestyles and modes of communication, demands wholly new ideas and analogies, classifications and concepts."

Given that the reputation of any futurologist hangs on the accuracy of their predictions, it is instructive to examine how elements of Toffler's view of the future compares to what has actually unfolded over the past two decades:

- "The essence of Second Wave manufacture was the long 'run' of millions of identical standardized products. By contrast, the essence of Third Wave manufacture is the short run of partially or completely customized products," writes Toffler. *Mass production has increasingly yielded pride of place to the concept of mass customization, to the extent that the latter now dominates most traditional mass production industries such as car manufacture.*
- "The customer will become so integrated into the production process that we will find it more and more difficult to tell just who

is actually the consumer and who the producer," says Toffler. *Online banking services, and Amazon's customers contributing book reviews are just two examples where customers now routinely do "work" on behalf of companies they deal with.*

- Toffler believed that, as well as its traditional commercial focus, the organization of the future would be greatly concerned with a range of social, ecological, moral and political problems. *There has been no significant sign of this happening on a voluntary basis, despite or possibly due to the degree of change that has occurred within organizations.*

- "Machine synchronization shackled the human to the machine's capabilities and imprisoned all of social life in a common frame. It did so in capitalist and socialist countries alike. Now, as machine synchronization grows more precise, humans, instead of being imprisoned, are progressively freed," says Toffler. *He rightly predicted the demise of the traditional nine-to-five working day, and the move towards flexible working patterns, without necessarily picking up on the fact that growing numbers of organizations would move to 24/7 working patterns.*

- Toffler predicts the "de-massifying" of our culture. *The growth of tribalism, the expansion of local TV and radio media, and greater personalization of communication services, e.g. the availability of video-on-demand down telephone lines, all point to cultural fragmentation.*

- The Third Wave, he writes, "will produce anxiety and conflict as well as reorganization, restructuring, and – for some – rebirth into new careers and opportunities. The new systems will challenge all the old executive turfs, the hierarchies, the sexual role divisions, the departmental barriers of the past." *These "new systems" can be seen in a number of trends and phenomena that have impacted on working life over the past 20 years e.g. empowerment, process re-engineering, the flattening of hierarchies, downsizing, house-husbands, the demise of the job for life, and portfolio working.*

Toffler spends a significant chunk of *The Third Wave* exploring how organizations and organizational life might change. "Instead of clinging to a sharply specialized economic function, the corporation, prodded by criticism, legislation, and its own concerned executives, is becoming a multipurpose institution," he writes. He identifies five forces that will impact on organizations, namely changes in:

1  The physical environment.
2  The line-up of social forces.

3   The role of information.
4   Government organization.
5   Morality.

Reading *The Third Wave* 20 years after its first publication is a curious experience. On one hand, the book remains very contemporary in feel, and his profile of the new economy is a pretty close match. On the other hand, when he gets down to the level of describing the nuts and bolts of technology to come, the book seems remarkably dated. For example, at one point he goes into some detail to describe what a word processor is. Perhaps though, that should merely serve to remind us how rapidly wave upon wave of technological innovation has come at us, and how, as Shoshana Zuboff once wrote, "patterns of morality, sociality and feeling are evolving much more slowly than technology."

*The Third Wave* has proved to be a largely accurate depiction of a future that has now more or less reached us. Given the status it has achieved, it seems all the more remarkable that it is currently virtually impossible to locate a copy in a bookstore – either bricks-and-mortar or on-line. Maybe the future isn't what it used to be.

## The author

A former Washington correspondent and editor of *Fortune* magazine, Alvin Toffler is a highly respected futurologist. He has served briefly as a visiting professor at Cornell University and a visiting scholar at the Russell Sage Foundation. He holds five honorary degrees.

## Sources and further reading

Toffler, Alvin (1980) *The Third Wave*, Bantam, USA.

Toffler, Alvin (1970) *Future Shock*, Bantam, USA.
Close to three decades ago, Toffler anticipated the waves of anxiety that the technological revolution would engender in this ground-breaking exploration of what happens to people and society when overwhelmed by change.

Zuboff, Shoshana (1995) "The Emperor's New Workplace," *Scientific American*, September.

# BRUCE TULGAN

## *Work This Way*

### 1998

**F**arewell then, job for life. We have been told repeatedly that the traditional career is over. Most people believe it, but nobody really seems to know what is going to replace it. Bruce Tulgan's *Work This Way* is a guide to the post-jobs era that aims to provide a set of readily applicable strategies for prospering in an environment where many are intent on merely surviving.

Tulgan offers the five essential ingredients of a re-invented career:

1   *Learn voraciously.* The next generation of employees already has an insatiable appetite for information. According to Tulgan we need to:
    • create our own opportunities to learn – the traditional education system by itself is no longer enough;
    • take personal control of our post-school education by designing our own courses;
    • maximize all corporate training opportunities and turn everyday life into a learning lab;
    • turn job-hopping into a personal training program.
2   *Concentrate on relationships.* Relationships with individuals will be the most reliable institutions in the post-jobs era. We need to:
    • identify and seek out the real decision-makers;
    • turn every contact into a multiple contact;
    • identify and win over gatekeepers;
    • get on the right person's radar *then prove that we are more than a blip*;
    • take personal responsibility for keeping relationships fizzing.
3   *Add value continuously.* The most successful workers today are chameleon-like, day-to-day value adders who are flexible and adapt

well to changing circumstances. There are temps – the fastest growing category of employees – but temping is not just for clerical workers anymore but for doctors, lawyers, engineers, bankers, scientists, teachers, programmers, trapeze artists and any other type of worker you can think of.

4   *Be balanced.* Tulgan urges us to set clear priorities in our working and personal lives and then to live by them no matter what. He considers it essential to stay close to our deepest values and priorities such as quality, integrity, fulfillment and well-being.

5   *Take it one year at a time.* In a changing environment long-term goals are good but long-term planning is useless. Instead Tulgan encourages us to plan our lives and careers only one year at a time.

Tulgan's previous book, *Managing Generation X*, looked at the career issues facing the generational successors to the post-war Baby Boomers, i.e. those born between 1963 and 1981. He found a group of people who value individualism and personal empowerment and who seem well equipped to handle life in the post jobs era. *Work This Way* marks an extension of his range to embrace the challenges facing anybody who expects to be working on the other side of all those millennium celebrations.

Like Tom Peters, Tulgan fizzes with provocative ideas, and like Peters much of what he writes about will prove to be wrong. However, buried within *Work This Way* are some profound truths about the way things will be. The trick is to find them and to prepare ourselves accordingly.

### Reality check: organizations need flea-thinking individuals

The recent announcement by the UK police that they will in future employ informers on a formal basis, giving them contracts and putting them on PAYE, is one of the more eye-catching indicators that we now live in a working world increasingly dominated by the knowledge economy. Although we are still in the early stages of this knowledge revolution, we can already see evidence of its impact reflected in ever more volatile markets, and organizations large and small showing increasing uncertainty about future direction.

At an individual level, most of us are experiencing huge uncertainties about future career and job prospects. Given that only 47% of people of working age in the UK are in full-time permanent roles these days – a drop of around 20% in as many years – it's hardly surprising that "a job for life" seems like a leftover concept from a very different era.

So if the future world of work is destined to become ever more volatile, what can organizations and individuals do to give themselves a better than average chance of survival? Charles Handy, writing in the October 1999 edition of *CBI News*, predicts that we are heading towards "a world of fleas and elephants, of large conglomerates and small individual entities" in which "elephants are a guarantee of continuity but fleas provide the innovation." So perhaps what organizations, regardless of size, will need more than anything is to acquire is a new mindset – an ability to think like a flea. Charles Leadbeater and Kate Oakley, in their recent pamphlet *The Independents* (Demos, 1999), give some examples of "flea thinking":

- *Be prepared to have several goes.* You're unlikely to make it first time around. Learn from failure, don't wallow in it.
- *Timing is critical.* Technology is moving so fast it's easy to be either too early or too late.
- *Don't have a plan.* It will come unstuck because it's too inflexible.
- *Have an intuition and a feel for where the market is headed.* Adapt and change with the consumers.
- *Be brave enough to be distinctive.* If you are doing what everyone else is doing, you're in the wrong business.
- *Be passionate.* If you don't believe in what you are doing, nobody else will. At the outset only passion will persuade other people to back you.
- *Make work fun.* If it stops being fun, people will not be creative.
- *Keep your business lean.* Buy top-of-the-range computers but put them on second-hand desks. Necessity is the mother of invention.
- *Give your employees a stake in the business.* You may not be able to pay them much to start with so give them shares.
- *Pick partners who are as committed as you.* To start with, a business will only be sustained by a band of believers.
- *Don't be sentimental.* Be ready to split with your partners – often your best friends – when the business faces a crisis or a turning point.
- *Take a holiday in Silicon Valley.* You will be convinced anyone is capable of anything.

Of course, the essence of flea-thinking is that this list will inevitably be overtaken by a new and better version. Maybe then the best we can do – individually and organizationally – is to have in place our own set of "copper's narks" – sources of information and knowledge about the future that will enable us to make truly informed choices.

## The author

Bruce Tulgan has written extensively on life in the new economy. He has produced five books to date.

## Sources and further reading

Bruce Tulgan (1998) *Work This Way: Inventing Your Career in the Workplace of the Future*, Capstone, UK.

Tulgan, Bruce (2000) *Managing Generation X* (2nd cdn), WW Norton, USA.

Crainer, Stuart (2000) *A Freethinker's A–Z of the New World of Business*, Capstone, UK.
Tulgan contributes to this book, which sets out to identify who/what are the major players shaping the new emerging business landscape. The vignettes on each topic are brief and pungent. Nearly all are supported by further sources of information, typically a Website or two – which is great for delving deeper where you need to.

# WATTS WACKER & JIM TAYLOR

## *The Visionary's Handbook*

## 2000

I t doesn't seem that far back in the corporate timeline when change used to happen in bursts, if at all. Occasionally, if you remember, a new CEO would have a rush of blood and personally re-design the business on the back of attending an executive seminar, perhaps bringing in some consultants to help. Senior managers would sigh, brace themselves for a few bumpy months and look forward to a time when life in the company would settle down again. Then, say in the mid to late eighties, companies realized they would have to flick the change switch onto constant and things would never be quite the same again.

And now, with constant change absorbed as an unquestioned given on most corporate agendas, post-millennial business life in the hinterlands of the new economy is due for another shake-up, say Watts Wacker and Jim Taylor in this gripping and mind-boggling book. Forget constant change, and embrace what the authors call constant paradox – a continuous collision of opposites that will affect us and the terms of our business and personal lives every moment we are alive.

In fact, Wacker and Taylor identify nine paradoxes in all covering everything from value and time to competition, action, leadership and leisure.

To help readers get to grips with the implications of these paradoxes, Wacker and Taylor offer practical examples to illuminate their meaning, as well as numerous exercises and reflection points to enable readers to chart their personal course for the future. But *The Visionary's Handbook* provides no glib, pre-packaged solutions. This is one of the book's virtues, say the authors:

"We admit it up front: We don't know your problems. We don't know the solutions, either. We can't, in either case. Your reality and our reality have many points in common because we share the same fundamental base of experience and sensory stimulation and because we live in the same moment in space and time, but our reality and yours are not now and never will be parallel. All we know are the questions you need to be asking, and all we can sense is that if you have picked up this book and read this far in it, you must be feeling something like the same uneasiness that sent us on our journey. Maybe your business feels out of control, or your career. Maybe it's your life generally that's on the edge. You don't know your problem, nor do we. We don't know your solution, nor do you. "

A bold, thought-provoking book, *The Visionary's Handbook* captures the interlocking web of paradoxes that abound in business life, and provides a map to help make the future work for every individual and every company in the challenging and uncertain times ahead.

## The nine paradoxes

### The paradox of value: intrinsic worth isn't

"The value of any product becomes inseparable from a buyer's perception of worth. Instead of intrinsic value, we have relative value only – the products that a business makes bear diminished relations to the physical content of the offering."

### The paradox of size: the bigger you are, the smaller you need to be.

"To operate effectively in a world in which each individual is a microculture and to communicate effectively and directly to the interests of those microcultures, you have to, in effect, atomize your organization and miniaturize its units."

### The paradox of time: At the speed of light, nothing happens

"To succeed in the short term, you need to think in the long term. Yet the greater your vision and the longer the time interval over which you predict results, the greater the risk that you will be unable to take the necessary steps in the short term to achieve the long-term goals. The tension between short- and long-term planning has never been more tormented."

### The paradox of competition: your biggest competitor is your own view of your future

"Competition comes from everywhere and nowhere at the same time. Competition needs to be viewed in both external and internal terms. Competition takes place in all three tenses."

### The paradox of action: you've got to go for what you can't expect to get

"Nothing will turn out exactly as it's supposed to. You must act intuitively and be equally ready to take resolute counterintuitive action."

### The paradox of leadership: to lead from the front, you have to stay inside the story

"In an inherently inconsistent world, consistency is not the virtue it once was in our leaders."

### The paradox of leisure: relax, dammit; play is hard work

"Play and work are blending and becoming indistinguishable."

*The paradox of the visionary: our reality is yours alone*

"The closer your vision gets to a provable truth, the more you are simply describing the present. In the same way, the more certain you are of a future outcome, the more likely you will be wrong."

*The paradox of reality: your reality is ours alone*

"Every person on planet Earth today has the potential to be connected to every other person, and every single one of us inhabits a world of our own and is a marketing segment of absolutely one. As our links become stronger, our individuation becomes starker."

Taken from *The Visionary's Handbook*

## The authors

Watts Wacker is a futurist at a leading think tank in the US.

Jim Taylor is a lecturer and consultant.

Howard means is a novelist and senior editor of the *Washingtonian*.

## Sources and further reading

Wacker, Watts, and Taylor, Jim, with Means, Howard (2000) *The Visionary's Handbook*, HarperBusiness, USA.

Taylor, Jim and Wacker, Watts, with Means, Howard (1997) *The 500 Year Delta*, Capstone, UK.
Every 500 years or so, say Taylor and Wacker, civilization encounters a period of change so vast and sweeping that nothing remains the same as before. In this highly unconventional yet absorbing book, they argue that we are now seeing the simultaneous collapse of the logical, social and economic assumptions we have lived by for the past 500 years. Drawing on the strategies and actions of various forward-looking individuals and fast companies, *The 500 Year Delta* pinpoints some fundamental practices that people will need to adopt.

# MICHAEL J. WOLF

## *The Entertainment Economy*

## 1999

**M**ichael Wolf knows a lot about media and entertainment. After all he founded and heads the Media and Entertainment practice at Booz-Allen & Hamilton in New York and has spent the last ten years consulting with the media moguls who head up the world's largest entertainment companies.

In *The Entertainment Economy*, he argues that media and entertainment have moved beyond mere culture to become the driving force of the global retail economy. As he puts it, "There's no business without show business." In this world where "entertainment content has become a key differentiator in virtually every aspect of the broader consumer economy," all consumer businesses need to acknowledge the multi-level relationships that entertainment businesses set out to build with their customers. In other words, in a world where businesses compete primarily for the time and attention of customers, content becomes king, and the quality of the experience the clincher.

However, perhaps the most useful insight of this book is that not all businesses will, or should, adopt an entertainment-based approach. As consumers look to satisfy more complex emotional needs, they become increasingly reluctant to waste time on lower-order ones. Wolf argues that retail will split into two paths: one headed towards entertainment venues, the other headed towards convenience. For companies on the latter path, convenience, price and consistent quality rather than entertainment remain the key variables. To buy a regular, no-frills item like a T-shirt, most consumers will go for a low-hassle, low-cost solution which might involve spending a few minutes in their chosen store. Even better, they are increasingly saving themselves the trouble of going out at all by ordering it over the Internet

---

**Zeitbite**

"Suits versus creatives was the old model. I feel that 'creative suits' is the new one."

Michael Wolf, *The Entertainment Economy*

---

This book is a compelling read for anyone who is even remotely interested in the media and entertainment world. Its great strength is that Michael Wolf is a real industry insider who continually engages the reader with examples and stories from across the industry. However, the danger is that the book's conversational style and entertainment-centric focus might mislead people into viewing it as an enjoyable and insightful read rather than a groundbreaking work with the potential to speak to a wider audience. *The Entertainment Economy* has some valid and highly relevant messages for the business world, but the book's lack of charts, tables, graphs, or even any bullet points means that extracting these messages requires quite a bit of work on the business reader's part.

## Ideas into action

Going to watch a movie is an experience that can fall into a number of different categories. At one level, it might simply while away a couple of hours on a rainy day in a warm and comfortable environment; at another level, the movie might arouse curiosity or amuse us; at yet another level, a movie can change the way we think or feel about something. In other words, a movie can engage an audience at a number of different levels.

This is not a totally novel concept. In a sense, the behavioral psychologist Abraham Maslow predicted this when he drew up his theory of motivation and stated that people's needs fall into a hierarchy. Basic needs such as food, warmth and shelter are at the bottom, more complex emotional needs in the middle, and "self actualization" at the top. As each need is satisfied, people move up to the next.

The challenge to businesses is to move their products and services up the hierarchy. Take Starbucks as a shining example; it has created an entire experience out of drinking coffee within an industry that was increasingly commoditized and price driven.

## High concept – from USP to UBP

"In recent years, Hollywood has embraced the notion of 'high concept': a compelling idea expressed in one simple thought.

" 'It's *Clueless* meets *Dumb and Dumber*' equals *There's Something About Mary* (last summer's surprise blockbuster); this is an example of a good high concept.

" 'High concept' brings to mind an idea at the foundation of modern advertising that was put forward in 1961 by Rosser Reeves when he was chairman of Ted Bates & Company. In his seminal work, *Reality in Advertising,* he stated that for a product to find its way in the marketplace, it was necessary to create a "unique selling proposition," or USP. According to Reeves, 'The USP almost lifts itself out of the ruck and wings its way to some corner of the mind … The USP leaps out at you!'

"This concept still holds true today, although, in the entertainment economy, I would turn it somewhat on its head and speak of a 'unique buying proposition': What is the deep-down reason that a consumer buys a product? Find the reason and you will understand what creates a hit, or even a phenomenon.

"In publishing, no high concept that has come along is more fundamental than the one behind the phenomenon that relationship guru John Gray kicked off with *Men are from Mars, Women are from Venus.* Simply stated, his idea is that 'Guys are different from girls, and here's why.' Gray's book sought to bridge the communication gap between the sexes, a fact of modern life that is apparent to anyone who has or has had a relationship with a member of the opposite sex. The book became a gigantic hit when it crossed over to a male audience and has sold more than 6.5 million copies.

"The marketers at HarperCollins realized they had a breakout hit on their hands that was driven by a high, but seemingly simple, concept. The hit became a phenomenon when, recognizing what was happening, the publisher pulled out all the marketing stops. Sequel books – ten of them – followed, as did audio tapes, CD-ROMS, videos, a Website, couples counseling, seminars, relationship cruises, even a Broadway show. *Men are from Mars, Women are from Venus* is a very good example of how a unique yet simple idea with all the right elements of hit building can, when the time and the public's mood are right, become a transforming phenomenon."

Taken from The Entertainment Economy

## The author

Michael J. Wolf is a senior partner in the New York-based Media and Entertainment Practice at Booz-Allen & Hamilton, a unit that he set up in 1991.

## Sources and further reading

Wolf, Michael J. (1999) *The Entertainment Economy: the Mega-Media Forces that are Shaping our Lives*, Random House, USA.

Pine, B. Joseph and Gilmore, James H. (1999) *The Experience Economy: Goods and Services are No Longer Enough*, Harvard Business School Press, USA.

# SHOSHANA ZUBOFF

## *In the Age of the Smart Machine*

## 1988

S o what can a book about technology written in the 1980s and based on research conducted up to a decade before that tell us about business life in the 21st Century?

The answer is "plenty." *In the Age of the Smart Machine* is a real rarity – a 20-year-old technology classic. Zuboff achieves this feat by concentrating less on the technology itself and more on its meaning and potential.

*In the Age of the Smart Machine* sets out to document the pitfalls and promise of computerized technology in business life. Picking through the book brings out a number of key themes, most of which still have great relevance today. Zuboff, for example, touches on all of the following issues, either explicitly or implicitly:

- Information technologies can transform work at every organizational level by having the potential to give all employees a comprehensive or near comprehensive view of the entire business. These technologies will surrender knowledge to anyone with the requisite skills. This contrasts with earlier generations of technological advance where the primary impact of new machines was to decrease the complexity of tasks.
- Information technologies can potentially increase the intellectual content of work at all levels. Work involves an ability to understand, respond to, manage, and create value from information. The most effective organizations will be those that achieve a more equitable distribution of knowledge and authority.
- Information technology presents us with a fateful choice: do we use it to continue automation at the risk of robbing workers of gratification and self image, or to empower ordinary working people to make judgments?

- Unlocking the promise of information technology depends on dismantling managerial hierarchies that all too often seek to block the ready flow of information.
- Information technology has the capacity not only to change where knowledge and power reside in the organization; it also changes time. The "working day" has less meaning in a global village where communication via electronic mail, voice mail, and facsimile transmissions can be sent or received at any time of day or night.
- Paradoxically, as the working day has expanded, so time has contracted. Companies compete on speed, using effective co-ordination of resources to reduce the time needed to develop new products, deliver orders or react to customer requests.
- Even more dramatically, new information technologies offer the possibility of restructuring whole industry sectors. Traditional value chain structures are fragmenting and reforming. Zuboff predicted the emergence of "virtual" organizations.
- If a company can replace an employee with a computer program that does not demand an ever-increasing salary, a pension, cheap mortgage or insurance, the danger is that it will. As a consequence, people can lose their outdated jobs almost overnight and remain unemployable because they lack the variety of skills and mental flexibility to adjust.
- As with the original industrial revolution, there are bound to be winners and losers. For every empowered, delayered, nano-technology worker doing valuable work, there is another who has lost their job, and yet another tucked away in their technologically Neanderthal office putting in longer and longer hours doing more of the same work. Are we destined to live in a world where some people are permanently overworked while others are permanently underworked?

Perhaps the most crucial point she raised revolves around how we humans relate to technology. In the final analysis, technology's potential is limited primarily by the power of the human imagination. As B.F. Skinner once wrote, "The real question is not whether machines think, but whether men do."

Zuboff goes further, arguing in a *Scientific American* article that technological capability has galloped ahead of our ability to cope because "so far, patterns of morality, sociality, and feeling are evolving much more slowly than technology."

The impact of information technology on organizations over the past 20 years or so has been huge. By enabling the creation of a global marketplace, and by decentralizing control and empowering people all along the information chain, technology redefines what is possible for organizations. New computer-based systems dissolve conventions of ownership, design, manufacturing, executive style, and national identity. This has profound implications for organizations.

Perhaps though, based on Zuboff's considerable insights, the most vital question that we need to address is whether, as technology surges further and further ahead, we are still at heart emotional Luddites.

## Zuboff on the informated workplace

"The informated workplace, which may no longer be a 'place' at all, is an arena through which information circulates, information to which intellective effort is applied. The quality, rather than the quantity, of effort will be the source from which added value is derived. Economists may continue to measure labor productivity as if the entire world of work could be represented adequately by the assembly line, but their measures will be systematically indifferent to what is most valuable in the informated organization. A new division of learning requires another vocabulary – one of colleagues and co-learners, of exploration, experimentation, and innovation. jobs are comprehensive, tasks are abstractions that depend upon insight and synthesis, and power is a roving force that comes to rest as dictated by function and need. A new vocabulary cannot be invented all at once – it will emerge from the practical action of people struggling to make sense in a new 'place' and driven to sever their ties with an industrial logic that has ruled the imaginative life of our century.

"The informated organization is a learning institution, and one of its principal purposes is the expansion of knowledge – not knowledge for its own sake (as in academic pursuit), but knowledge that comes to reside at the core of what it means to be productive. Learning is no longer a separate activity that occurs either before one enters the workplace or in remote classroom settings. Nor is it an activity preserved for a managerial group. The behaviors that define learning and the behaviors that define being productive are one and the same. Learning is not something that requires time out from being engaged in productive activity; learning is the heart of productive activity. To put it simply, learning is the new form of labor.

"The precise contours of a new division of learning will depend upon the business, products, services, and markets that people are engaged in learning about. The empowerment, commitment, and involvement of a wide range of organizational members in self-managing activities means that organizational structures are likely to be both emergent and flexible, changing as members continually learn more about how to organize themselves for learning about their business. However, some significant conceptual issues are raised by the prospect of a new division of learning in the informated organization. The following discussion of these issues does not offer a rigid prescription for practice but suggests the kinds of concrete choices that define an informating strategy."

Extracted from *In the Age of the Smart Machine*

## The author

Shoshana Zuboff is a Professor at the Harvard Business School. She has written extensively about how computers will affect the future of work.

## Sources and further reading

Zuboff, Shoshana (1988) *In the Age of the Smart Machine: the Future of Work and Power*, Basic Books, USA.

Zuboff, Shoshana (1995) "The Emperor's New Workplace," *Scientific American*, September.

# Annotated Bibliography

ife, as we know, is rarely neat. So it should surprise nobody that there were a number of books over and above the 50 that comprise the body of *Writing the New Economy* that came close to being included. Here are some of the best.

## Mastering the Digital Marketplace: Practical Strategies for Competitiveness in the New Economy
Douglas F. Aldrich
John Wiley, 2000

In the digital economy, argues Aldrich, there are two key measures of value: time (as in how much time your product or service will save the customer); and content (information, knowledge, or services that provide added value to the customer). He goes on to outline a new business model which he calls the Digital Value Network (DVN), a community of electronically linked business partners that work together to produce value for the customer as the customer defines it, and offers strategies for creating and sustaining it. This dynamic, fluid entity will have the ability to form, disintegrate, and reform based on market dynamics and the whims of the customer, and will be the hallmark of the successful organizations of the future. An intriguing business model, and Aldrich makes a compelling case for it becoming a blueprint for success in the digital revolution.

### The Meme Machine
Susan Blackmore
Oxford University Press, 1999

Once humans learned to receive, copy and retransmit memes – a meme being in essence a captivating idea, behavior, or skill that can be transferred from one person to another by imitation – the rest, says Blackmore, is a foregone conclusion. Memetic competition shapes our minds and culture, just as natural selection has shaped our physical evolution. But why should this matter to us and the organizations we work for? Well, for a start, it explains why the sexual adventures of an errant senior manager would grip the corporate imagination more than the latest set of financial figures. Blackmore explores her subject with great panache. Some readers who like to explore both sides of an argument before making up their own minds may find her sure-footed advocacy a little overpowering, but for the rest of us *The Meme Machine* is a riveting and provocative read.

### The Electronic B@zaar
Robin Bloor
Nicholas Brealey, 2000

Bloor's mix of leading-edge IT analysis, historical perspective, and a sound grasp of economic principles makes for an informative and entertaining account of the new economic landscape. *The Electronic B@zaar* occasionally reads as though it has been put through some kind of Tom Peters style-writer software, but nonetheless the book is a compelling call to arms for anybody seeking practical tips about making the transition from bricks-and-mortar to successful e-business.

### Knowledge Capitalism
Alan Burton-Jones
Oxford University Press, 1999

Burton-Jones marshals an impressive range of evidence in this closely argued exploration of how the shift to a knowledge-based economy is redefining the shape and nature of organizations. He also describes the emergence of a new breed of capitalist, one dependent on knowledge rather than physical resources. There are plenty of easier reads about the knowledge economy on the market, but those looking for substance rather than eye-catching glibness will be pleased to find in *Knowledge Capitalism* a book that provides frequent moments of insight without compromising gravitas.

### Portfolio People
Max Comfort
Century Business Books, 1997

Charles Handy is generally credited for "inventing" the idea of the work portfolio – a way of describing how the different bits of work in our life can fit together – in *The Age of Unreason*. Since that book's publication in 1989, increasing numbers of people are finding that, either through choice or necessity, they have portfolio careers. Max Comfort provides a lively and accessible guide to the subject, reporting on the personal experiences of Portfolio People, and encouraging readers to consider – through questionnaires and reflective exercises – how equipped they are to take up a portfolio career.

### Executive EQ
Robert Cooper & Ayman Sawaf
Orion Business Books, 1997

Daniel Goleman's best-selling *Emotional Intelligence*, published in 1996, claims that our emotions play a much greater role in thought, decision making and individual success than is commonly acknowledged. Executive EQ (the initials stand for emotional quotient) argues that emotional intelligence will be a new driving force in business. Whether this will prove to be the case is open to question – most organizations are still not noted for their emotional maturity – but this is a self-help book with enough business examples to give the idea credibility. Readers have the opportunity to map their own emotional intelligence by completing a questionnaire at the back of the book.

### The Living Company
Arie de Geus
Nicholas Brealey, 1997

Drawing on unpublished research conducted by Shell in the early 1980s, Arie de Geus – the man widely credited for originating the concept of the "learning organization" – believes that most companies fail because they focus too narrowly on financial performance and pay insufficient attention to themselves as communities of human beings with the potential to learn, adapt and grow. The living company, he says, emphasizes knowledge rather than capital, and adaptability rather than core competencies. De Geus won the Edwin G Booz prize for Most Insightful Management Book back in 1997 and so it is a little disappointing that his ideas have not yet broken through into the mainstream. Nonetheless, anybody with an interest in organizational learning will find something of value here. Highly recommended.

### In the Company of Giants
Rama Dev Jager & Rafael Ortiz
McGraw-Hill, 1997

Described by the authors as a set of "candid conversations with the visionaries of the digital world," the book comprises transcripts of 15 interviews, each one preceded by a brief pen picture of the interviewee. Those featured include Bill Gates, Andy Grove, Bill Hewlett, and Michael Dell, and so the book does live up to its title. Although there are some useful tidbits and quotable responses to questions, the book also serves to demonstrate how much things have changed in the three years since *In the Company of Giants* was published.

### Post-Capitalistic Society
Peter Drucker
HarperCollins, 1993

An early picture of new economy which has held up extremely well over the intervening years. Tom Peters may be the most famous living management guru, but Drucker is probably the most respected and insightful.

### StrikingItRich.com
Jaclyn Easton
McGraw-Hill, 1999

Subtitled *Profiles of 23 Incredibly Successful Companies You've Probably Never Heard Of*, Jaclyn Easton's rigorously researched and extremely readable book proves that Websites don't have to be high-profile extravaganzas to make serious money. The sites featured demonstrate that it is perfectly possible for a Website to achieve a profit quickly if an idea is well conceived and executed and if start-up costs are managed tightly. There is a companion Website at www.StrikingItRich.com.

### Entrepreneurship and the Wired Life: Work in the Wake of Careers
Fernando Flores & John Gray
Demos, 2000

The career, as an institution, is in unavoidable decline according to this fascinating pamphlet from independent UK think tank Demos. The authors describe two work patterns – the Wired and the Entrepreneurial – which might replace the traditional career work pattern. In a nutshell, the Wired life/work pattern replaces the lifelong identity of the career with a series of "brief habits," at the heart of which is spontaneity rather than continuity of projects and relationships. With the Entrepreneurial life/work pattern, Flores and Gray widen out the narrow economic definition of entrepreneurship to include all manner of activities which initiate meaningful change in a context of shared responsibility. This could be in commerce, service or in society in general. The authors go on to examine these new forms of working life in some detail and consider the implications for individuals and communities. They conclude that core institutions – from education to pensions – need restructuring to support these changes. At only 48 pages long, *Entrepreneurship and the Wired Life* is that rare phenomenon – a business book that could usefully have been double the length.

### Getting a Life
Polly Ghazi & Judy Jones
Hodder & Stoughton, 1997

In *Getting a Life*, Ghazi and Jones provide a good insight into the downshifting movement. In the first half of the book they deal with conceptual matters; the roots of movement in the US, the marked changes in employment and employability over the last decade and the current British experience with downshifting. In the second half they turn to the practical matters of how to downshift. Here they cover not only the financial essentials but a broad array of topics including health, feng shui, and our contribution to community. If you are one of those people who refuse to see the world in terms of black or white but prefer shades of grey, this book is for you. The world, it turns out, is not composed of "downshifters" and conventional employees. We are not forced to choose between the two. It is, rather, a question of which elements of the downshifting movement we might like to incorporate into our lives.

### The Tipping Point: How Little Things Can Make a Big Difference
Malcolm Gladwell,
Little, Brown, 2000

Why do some minority tastes remain strictly minority, while others extend into the mainstream? Although Gladwell, a journalist rather than an academic, makes no reference to Richard Dawkins' concept of memes or to Kevin Kelly's law of plentitude, this well written and racy exploration covers similar terrain, i.e. what lies behind the point when a small fad acquires critical mass and takes off. *The Tipping Point* is very readable but the central idea isn't really enough to sustain a whole book – no surprise then to discover that it began its life as a long article in *New Yorker* magazine.

### Net Gain
John Hagel III & Arthur G. Armstrong.
Harvard Business School Press, 1997

Well-written and insightful view of the new economy. focusing on how virtual communities can expand markets. Highly recommended by Kevin Kelly in his bibliography at the back of *New Rules for the New Economy*.

### The New Century
Eric Hobsbawm
Little, Brown, 2000

In which the pre-eminent historian (you won't find a better account of the 20th century than his *Age of Extremes*) offers his analysis of the current state of the world. Although the scope of this book goes much wider than the new economy, there's one chapter in particular – called

"The global village" – that offers a lucid, cool-headed, and reasoned assessment of the global economy. It's a much-needed antidote to the starry-eyed hyperbole that seems to dominate the globalization debate.

### On the Edge
Will Hutton & Anthony Giddens
Jonathan Cape, 2000

*On the Edge* draws together ten original contributions by leading thinkers like Paul Volcker, Manuel Castells, Arlie Russell Hochschild and George Soros. Overall conclusion seems to be that global capitalism does have huge potential for good but is just as likely to create a set of consequences that most of us would rather avoid. Co-author and Industrial Society boss Will Hutton describes global capitalism as "precarious and potentially dangerous." An important book that takes a clear-eyed view of its subject.

### Starting and Running a Business on the Internet
Tim Ireland
Take That Ltd, 2000

Coming in at just 109 pages and at a quarter of the cost of similar books, *Starting and Running a Business on the Internet* is an admirably concise and accessible guide for those wanting to know the practical steps involved in setting up a successful Internet business, from first conception through to promoting the site. A cautionary note, though. Ireland's particular strength rests in his knowledge of the mechanics of setting up a new Internet business – from acquiring a domain name, through to "going live" and taking orders from around the world. He does not set out to provide a comprehensive guide to the overall business start-up process and so readers will find nothing on raising capital, hiring staff, business planning *et al.* These reservations aside, this book is a useful *vade mecum* for the would-be Internet entrepreneur.

### Simplicity
Bill Jensen
HarperCollins, 2000

One of the few books written from the knowledge worker's perspective.

Jam-packed with tools and techniques for the individual, but also contains some useful insights on to how to build corporate infrastructures so the company is the tool of the worker, not the other way around. Also worth checking out www.simplerwork.com, the companion Website.

## Wired Life
Charles Jonscher
Anchor, 1999

Lord Reith's goal for the BBC was that it should inform, educate and entertain. Harvard academic and successful businessman Jonscher achieves this mix brilliantly in *Wired Life*. Neither Luddite nor technophile in outlook, Jonscher takes a clear-eyed look at the digital age and argues convincingly that the human spirit must be master of, and not slave to, the new information technologies.

## The One Best Way
Robert Kanigel
Little, Brown, 1997

*The One Best Way* is an illuminating biography of Frederick W. Taylor, the efficiency expert and "the father of scientific management." Although he lived through little of it – he died in 1915, aged 59 – Taylor's influence on the 20th century is unquestionable. Peter Drucker, for example, rates him alongside Freud and Darwin as a maker of the modern world. And despite its critics, Taylorism lives on, whether in the form of re-engineering (a direct descendant of scientific management), the continuing debate about the de-skilling of jobs, or the global standardization of companies like McDonald's. In his closing comments, Kanigel neatly sums up Taylor's impact on the world of work:

> "The coming of Taylorism made our age what it was going to become anyway – only more so, more quickly, more irrevocably. Taylor died relatively young. But he lived long enough to take currents of thought drifting through his own time – standards, order, production, regularity, efficiency – and codify them into a system that defines our age.
> "In its thrall, and under its blessing, we live today."

At 570 pages, the book is definitely top-heavy with detail. However, as an introduction to arguably the world's first management consultant, it makes fascinating reading.

## The Complexity Advantage
Susanne Kelly & Mary Ann Allison
McGraw Hill, 1999

This book argues that anybody operating in a business world growing ever more complex would benefit from an understanding of complexity theory. *The Complexity Advantage* represents a serious and sustained attempt to incorporate complexity principles and methodologies into business thinking. The more general reader may initially be baffled by some of the terminology but intelligent persistence will pay off.

## Community Building on the Web
Amy Jo Kim
Peachpit Press, 2000

A thriving Website, according to Kim, is one that engages people and makes them want to return time and time again. Those that encourage the participation of visitors go beyond simply offering a source of information and provide a platform for visitors, or community members, to meet and exchange thoughts and ideas. Kim's practical knowledge of building online communities comes over strongly, her tips and advice convincing and her enthusiasm infectious. The book has a companion Website which can be found at www.naima.com/community

## Open Minds
Andy Law
Orion, 1998

St Luke's is a high-profile London-based advertising agency and Andy Law has been the company's iconoclastic chairman since 1995. Owned entirely by its employees, all physical resources – offices, PCs etc. – in the company are shared, and there is little hierarchy. Employees are involved in almost all decisions, including setting their own pay rises. Whether the model developed at St Luke's has the resilience to cope with a downturn in its business fortunes (the company has enjoyed continuous growth since its creation) remains to be seen. In the meantime,

*Open Minds* makes a compelling case study, describing and explaining as it does the business practices and philosophy behind this fascinating company.

### The Soul of the New Consumer
David Lewis & Darren Bridger
Nicholas Brealey, 2000

A fascinating exploration by two consumer researchers of ways in which the new economy is changing not only *how* we buy but also *what* we buy and *why*. The New Consumers of the book's title are redefining the marketplace by defying traditional marketing concepts and segmentation by age, gender or income. So how should companies set about wooing this new breed of customers? Forget "the customer is king" say the authors – the way to win the attention, time and trust of New Consumers is to "give their souls control."

### Trusted Partners
Jordan Lewis
Free Press, 1999

Mergers and alliances on an ever grander scale are a feature of the global economy. *Trusted Partners* describes how to build trust between organizations that are forging alliances of various types with other companies, and explores how interpersonal relationships are a critical element of that. Drawing on experience built over four decades of working with some of the world's leading companies, Lewis goes well beyond theoretical analysis of the nature of trust between corporate "rivals" to lay out some practical and eminently sensible steps involved in building and maintaining trust.

### Understanding Media
Marshall McLuhan
Sphere, 1964

Marshall McLuhan's investigation into the state of the then emerging mass media is an exuberant, provocative, and scatter-gun piece of work. Much of the challenge he made to sixties' sensibilities and assumptions about how and what we communicate still holds good. *Understanding*

*Media* reads like a work in progress that connects to the new economy in the same way that H.G. Wells linked to the Apollo moon landings.

## The Death of Competition
James F. Moore.
HarperCollins, 1996

Business as ecosystem – Moore explores the biological metaphor in great detail and with considerable insight. One of the first and arguably the best exploration of leadership and strategy in a future that Moore envisions will be characterized by organized chaos.

## World class: Thriving Locally in the Global Economy
Rosabeth Moss Kanter
Simon and Schuster, 1995

Professor Moss Kanter tackles big issues in this book: globalization, the future of capitalism, communitarianism, xenophobia, and cultural imperialism. It is a disquieting book – her world is one in which the new colonialism will be brought about by a techno-elite. When she does stop to consider the human side to all this, it is to conclude that sensible xenophobics should see the error of their ways and realize that globalization can only do them good. This is an important book because it comes from a woman who has access to very good data indeed, a woman who ought to know. But if her reading of the rise of the new world class is accurate, this is also a very scary book. The global economy promises global dystopia.

## Computer Lib
Theodor H. Nelson
Microsoft Press International, 1988

Ted Nelson, part-academic, part-computer visionary, is generally credited with coining the term "hypertext" and putting it to work as a new mode of publication in the emerging computer technologies of the sixties and seventies. He also conceived a system called Xanadu, recognizably a fore-runner of the World Wide Web, where electronic documents are linked up. Great book by a true visionary and a true pleasure to read – so why is it out of print? Despite this snub from the publishing world, Nelson retains a loyal following and it is maybe only natural that the best sources of information about him are Internet-based. If you're interested, try www.xanadu.com

### Reality Hacking
Nicola Phillips
Capstone, 1997

It's an indication of this book's general approach that readers are invited to start and finish reading it anywhere they like. Using a mixture of provocative questions and inspirational quotes, and working from the principle that "the best way to enjoy your future is to invent it yourself," Phillips encourages the reader to reconsider their assumptions about their work and their life. Some will find this book inspirational and life-changing, others will dismiss it as pretentious psychobabble. That both groups have a point is a paradox that Phillips would relish.

### The Soul of the Internet
Neil Randall
Thomson Computer Press, 1997

The history of the Internet as told by many of the individuals involved in its development. Randall pulls the story together well, putting the Internet's development into its technological, social, educational and commercial contexts. What becomes clear from reading this substantial book is that the developers and builders of the Internet outnumber the true visionaries several times over.

### The Internet Start-Up Bible
Tess Read, Callum Chace & Simon Rowe
Random House, 2000

*The Internet Start-Up Bible* is an accessible, well-written guide about how to plan, research, fund, market and implement a successful Internet-based business model. The authors take the logical and too often neglected step of applying the same success criteria to dot.com business start-ups as to traditional ventures. Important sections on the entrepreneurial mindset, the process of shaping ideas into marketable concepts, and employing and managing people are included. Detailed chapters on business planning and attracting venture capital are followed by sections on various aspects of starting up an Internet business – technology, design, marketing and launch – before concluding with business growth and flotation. The book is crammed with useful case studies, extensive links, contact addresses, running quotes from business gurus and key books.

### Shakedown: How the New Economy is Changing our Lives
Angus Reid
Doubleday Publishing, 1997

As Chairman and CEO of the Angus Reid Group Inc., a leading Canadian polling firm, Angus Reid has been close to the dreams and aspirations of the Canadian people for close to 20 years. In *Shakedown* he describes how three major discontinuities are converging to change the shape of Canadian society for ever. The combination of technological change, globalization and the ageing of the population has meant the end of the "spend and share era" of national prosperity and optimism that characterized Canada from the 60s to the 80s and the beginning of a new uncertainty era which Reid christens the "sink or swim" era. The power of this book is in the detail; how these changes are affecting every aspect of Canadian life today and how they will shape the future. Although the book is written for Canadians, its message is universal and is one that we can all readily identify with.

### Soloing: Reaching Life's Everest
Harriet Rubin
Random House, London, 1999

Few of us can aspire to the heights of the people Rubin quotes, who retreat to stunning locations to think, and turn down all but the most fascinating jobs. That said, it's hard not to like this book. It is jam packed with practical ideas, unconventional wisdom and handy hints. And, apart from the worst cynics among us, who can resist anyone who insists that we must *learn* our livings? Maybe Rubin is right. Perhaps we can all arrive at the point where we "get so good at doing only what [we] love that work feels like play."

### *The Social Life of Information*
John Seely Brown & Paul Duguid
Harvard Business School Press, 2000

The authors put forward a convincing and eloquent argument that human sociability needs to play an important role in the digital world. They explore the importance of placing information in a social context, highlighting the dangers inherent in separating, in their words, "text from context." Their conclusion that the digital world stills needs a human heart at its center is both plausible and uplifting.

### *The Fifth Discipline*
Peter Senge
Business Books, 1990

Senge's book was one of the first to popularize the concept of the learning organization. His five core disciplines that underpin the building of a learning community are Personal Mastery, Mental Models (the filters through which we view the world), Shared Vision, Team Learning and Systems Thinking. The last of these, which Senge terms the cornerstone discipline, is covered in 70 pages in a section that represents an excellent generalist introduction to the main concepts of systems thinking, a core skill in a globalized, networked economy.

### *Customers.com*
Patricia Seybold
Random House, 1998

*Customers.com* offers practical and implementable advice based on the sound premise that any e-commerce initiative has to begin with the customer. The book contains some instructive case studies about how companies like Hertz, PhotoDisc, National Semiconductor, and Wells Fargo are using the Internet successfully. Shelfloads of books have now been written on this theme but what sets *Customers.com* apart is Seybold's talent for communicating her 20 years of experience in the technology industry in an accessible and no-nonsense writing style. Well worth checking out the second edition of the book, published in Autumn 2000.

## Silicon Gold Rush: the Next Generation of High-tech Stars Rewrites the Rules of Business
Karen Southwick
John Wiley, 1999

Southwick, managing editor of Forbes ASAP, takes us behind the scenes of 23 top-notch high-tech Silicon Valley companies, among them Cisco Systems, Yahoo!, Novell, and 3Com, and extracts what she terms the ten commandments for next-generation businesses. These are:

1 Shape the company's culture and work ethic.
2 Maintain a fresh perspective.
3 Cultivate knowledge.
4 Develop mind share.
5 Eschew formal structures and be a team.
6 The customer, not the technology, is #1.
7 Find the right partners, mergers, and acquisitions.
8 Embrace the unknown.
9 Be paranoid.
10 Be a speed demon and don't be squeamish.

In an influential industry where the rules of business are constantly being rewritten, *Silicon Gold Rush* provides a timely guide to the companies at the bleeding edge of technological advances.

## Profit Patterns
Slywotzky, Morrison, Moser, Mundt & Quella
John Wiley, 1999

A total re-questioning of different types of profit models is a necessary aspect of success in the new economy. In *Profit Patterns*, the authors introduce pattern thinking as a means of enabling managers to envision opportunities and design winning strategies ahead of the competition. "Like the best chess players," they write, "masters of business pattern recognition, instead of seeing chaos, know how to identify the strategic picture unfolding within the complexity and discover the pattern behind it all." The book describes a set of 30 patterns that have occurred in industry after industry, shifting billions of pounds in market value from those who "missed" them to those who "mastered" them. Company case studies that feature in the book include Dell, Microsoft and Amazon. Not an easy read particularly, but one that rewards attention.

*Twilight of Sovereignty*
Walt Wriston
Charles Scribner & Sons, 1992

Walt Wriston, former chairman of Citicorp, addresses the issues facing the corporations of America and the world during the 1990s and beyond. He argues that centralized corporate/political power has disappeared; that the world has been transformed by technology; and that negotiation will rule the world in future. Well worth a read (if you can track down a copy).

# Tracking the New Economy

or readers wanting to keep up to date with new economy developments, the following list of publications and Websites are worth dipping into on a regular basis:

## Business 2.0

Recently launched in the UK by Future Publishing, and with a strapline of "New economy • New Rules • New Leaders," *Business 2.0* is a monthly magazine that is jam-packed with intelligent and insightful articles. If it maintains the promise and high content level of its early issues, it could rapidly become a first port of call for students of the new economy.

## Business Intelligence

Publisher of some solid but very expensive reports (typically around £600 a copy). Website carries some useful free material though.
www.business-intelligence.co.uk/

## Centre for Business Innovation

Site managed by consultants Ernst and Young – quality of content varies but occasionally provokes thought.
www.businessinnovation.ey.com

## Economist

The best single source of information about what is happening in the world. A mainstream publication but one that will take on some big topics from time to time, and one whose take on the new economy is variably insightful and clear-eyed.

www.economist.com

## Fast Company

A US-published monthly magazine that has been an essential read since it started up in 1996. Of late, though, the content – while still excellent – has been swamped by increasing volumes of advertising. The companion Website is just about the best free site around on the new economy and the future world of work (it also carries material not found in the magazine).

www.fastcompany.com/home.html

## Financial Times

Of all the dailies, the *Financial Times* provides the best in-depth coverage of IT and work-related issues. Andy Hobsbawm's column – *@ The Chat Room* – in the Saturday *FT* is an invariably thought-provoking and topical look at various ways in which technology is impacting on our lives. Also well worth keeping an eye out for their occasional information technology surveys as well as their monthly e-business magazine *Connectis*.

www.ft.com
www.ft.com/connectis

## Fucked Company

An irreverent spoof of *Fast Company* that, like the very best Dilbert cartoons, uses humor as a vehicle for revealing some painful truths about working in the new economy.

www.fuckedcompany.com

## Future Filter

A subscription-only bi-monthly that sets out to be a business digest for the new economy. Excellent book review section.
www.futurefilter.com

## George Gilder's *Telecosm* Index

Originally due for publication in the mid-1990s and now expected towards the end of 2000, Gilder's book *Telecosm* has acquired an almost mythic status. Anybody interested in the present and future impact of technology on the US and world economy will find Gilder's articles for *Forbes* magazine an intriguing set of appetizers from this seminal thinker and iconoclast.
http://homepage.seas.upenn.edu/~gaj1/ggindex.html

## Harvard Business Review

Still the most authoritative business bi-monthly on the block. It has tended in the past to be more mainstream than truly groundbreaking in its coverage of business issues. That said, HBR has responded well to the challenge to traditional business thinking posed by the new economy, and recent issues have generally contained two or three relevant articles. Also, if you are interested in getting the lowdown on forthcoming books from Harvard's publishing wing several months before publication, the magazine consistently trails major books with articles from the authors. The Website provides overview of contents of the magazine – no free articles but the executive summaries are there and they are often all you need.
www.hbsp.harvard.edu/home.html

## (The) Information Economy

This Website is overseen by Economist Hal Varian, co-author of *Information Rules*, and lists hundreds of papers, works in progress, and links to other new economy Websites. An almost overwhelming resource but one that hasn't been bettered for thoroughness.
http://www.sims.berkeley.edu/resources/infoecon/

## Information Society Initiative

Sponsored by the UK government's Department of Trade and Industry, the Information Society Initiative is intended to encourage businesses to get involved in e-commerce. The Website contains informative material including some particularly useful (and free) CD-ROMs on the subject of doing business electronically.

www.isi.gov.uk

## *Internet Business*

Just about the best of the recent flurry of new monthlies about the doing business on the Internet. Informative mix of case studies, interviews, book extracts, and topical news stories.

## *New Scientist*

Important science and technology stories will often appear here first. *New Scientist* also gives good coverage to emerging thinking in the scientific community.

www.newscientist.com

## *New Thinking*

*New Thinking* is a weekly, approximately 500-word exploration of the digital age, produced by Gerry McGovern, CEO of Nua and author of *The Caring Economy*. Taking a broad, philosophical view of things, it is written in clear, concise language and delivers some useful comments and ideas. It is available by email and is free. To subscribe to this list, send email to: newthinking-request@nua.ie with the word *subscribe* in the body of the message.

## *Red Herring*

A monthly magazine that looks at the companies and trends that are shaping the business of technology. Although occasionally prone to obsess about the technology itself rather than the impact of the technology, *Red Herring* is nonetheless still worth an occasional scan.

www.redherringcom

## Revolution

UK-published weekly about business and marketing in the digital economy. More "newsy" than considered and analytical, it's nonetheless a good read and gives better coverage than any other daily or weekly.

## Start Up Failures

A Website that offers support to people who have joined the dot.com mania and failed. Although the site has been known to sell T-shirts bearing the motto "If disco can make a comeback, so can you," the overall intent is serious – visitors are offered the opportunity to share dot.com experiences as well as access to job listings for those keen to try again.

www.startupfailures.com

## Think Tanks

Good startpoint for exploring all the UK's major think tanks.

www.demos.co.uk/linkuk.htm

## The Utne Reader

A digest, whose editors scan thousands of small and alternative magazines. Not that well focused perhaps, but worth visiting for occasional gems.

www.utne.com

## Time

Weekly news magazine that gives good, positive coverage to new economy issues and people (Amazon's Jeff Bezos was their 1999 Person of the Year). That said, *Time* is a mainstream publication and so is unlikely to be absolutely at the forefront of new economy thinking. Nonetheless, it has in recent months carried special features on e-commerce, the future of work, and so on.

www.time.com/europe

## *Wired* magazine

Monthly American magazine that is good at picking up trends about six months before they become trends.

www.wired.com/wired/

## www.ecentre.com

A software shop for the more technically minded that helps users research e-business products.

## www.ecominfocenter.com

Good all round US e-commerce site full of good marketing tips plus some worthwhile links.

## www.e-comm.webopedia.com

Good startpoint for anybody baffled by the terms used in e-business.

# Glossary for the New Economy

**Adhocracy:** a non-bureaucratic networked organization with a highly organic organizational design.

**Affiliate marketing:** pioneered by the likes of Amazon and CDNow, anybody with a Website can sign up with them as a sales affiliate and receive a commission (typically 5%–15%) for any sales that are channeled through the affiliate site.

**Anoraknophobia:** an exaggerated, irrational fear of computers and the Internet. It derives from "anorak," a term once used to describe a person with trainspotting tendencies but which has evolved to embrace people obsessed with technology.

**Bricks and mortar:** companies that use traditional methods of selling and distributing products.

**Choiceboards:** interactive, on-line systems that let people design their own products from a menu of attributes, prices and delivery options.

Source: *Harvard Business Review*, January–February 2000

**Chumming:** The indiscriminate distribution of one's business card or e-mail address in the hope of attracting the interest of somebody important.

**Clusters:** critical masses in one place of linked industries that enjoy a high level of success in their particular field. Famous examples are Silicon Valley and Hollywood but clusters can be found everywhere. According to Michael Porter, clusters can affect competition in three ways:

1 by increasing the productivity of companies based in the area
2 by driving the direction and speed of innovation in their field
3 by stimulating the formation of new businesses within the cluster.

> Source: derived from an article called "Clusters and the
> new economics of competition" by Michael Porter,
> *Harvard Business Review*, November–December 1998

**Cluster geeking:** the process by which devoted fans of anything from Dr Who to Lego bricks form Internet communities to pursue their particular passion.

**Communities of practice:** groups that form within an organization, typically of their own accord, where members are drawn to one other by a common set of needs that may be both professional and social. Compared to project teams, communities of practice are voluntary, longer-lived, have no specific deliverable, and are responsible only to themselves. Because they are free of formal strictures and hierarchy within an organization, they can be viewed as subversive.

**Confusion marketing:** a process described by the UK Consumer Association as the way in which some businesses are seeking to deny customers the means of making an informed choice by swamping them with an excess of confusing price information. The intention is clear – to make price comparisons with rivals impossible in practical terms. The hope is that customers will give up in frustration and stay with or move to well-known companies or brands. Customers signing up for a mobile phone or obtaining a mortgage for house purchase in the UK are facing confusion marketing tactics.

**Core competents:** a relatively small number of executive high achievers increasingly hold corporate power. Shortages of executive talent mean that the truly talented will have their choice of the plum roles. Talented executives will be in demand and will be able to attract substantial salary and remuneration packages. In effect, corporate power will be concentrated in the hands of the few. "What is critical in the firm of the future is not so much the core competencies as the core competents," predicts Jonas Ridderstråle of the Stockholm School of Economics. "These walking monopolies will stay as long as the company can offer them something they want. When that is no longer the case, they'll leave."

Ridderstråle points to a growing array of supporting evidence. Bill Gates has reflected that if 20 people were to leave Microsoft, the company would risk bankruptcy. In a study by the Corporate

Leadership Council, a computer firm recognized 100 "core competents" out of 16,000 employees; a software company had 10 out of 11,000; and a transportation group deemed 20 of its 33,000 as really critical.

So few, yet so powerful. According to Randall E. Stross, professor of business at San Jose State University and a research fellow at Stanford University: "In the software industry, a single programmer's intellectual resources, through commercial alchemy, can create entire markets where none existed before. Compare the cumulative worldwide gross revenues of the studio that captures the next Steven Spielberg to the rival who has to settle for the second-round draft pick. Differences separating the rewards generated by the top tier versus the second tier are geometric, not arithmetic." At the top of the organization, that difference is likely to be exponential.

Source: Stuart Crainer (2000)
*A Freethinker's A-Z of the New World of Business*, Captone, UK

**Customer Relationship Management (CRM):** a set of techniques and approaches designed to provide personalized service to customers and to increase customer loyalty. Increasingly viewed as a strategic issue, and one that typically requires technological support.

**Customer sacrifice:** the gap between what customers settle for and what they really want. Successful companies reduce customer sacrifice by cultivating learning relationships. The more customers "teach" the company, the better it can provide just what they want – and the more difficult it becomes for competitors, to whom customers would have to teach their preferences afresh, to lure them away.

Source: B. Joseph Pine II and James H. Gilmore (1999)
*The Experience Economy*, Harvard Business School Press

**Cyberspace:** term originally coined by William Gibson in his book *Neuromancer*. Now generally used to describe the notional social arena we "enter" when using computers to communicate.

**Data marts:** scaled-down version of a data warehouse containing specific information of interest to a particular target group.

**Data mining:** the process of using advanced statistical tools to identify commercially useful patterns or relationships in databases.

**Data warehouse:** a database that can access all of a company's information.

**Desk rage:** long hours and the growing pressures of the workplace are leading to increasing outbreaks of office strife or "desk rage." As stress builds in the office, workers are increasingly venting their frustrations on colleagues.

**Disintermediation:** buzzword for how the Internet is cutting out the middlemen, enabling wholesalers/manufacturers to sell direct to the end user. Classic potential victims of disintermediation are estate agents and travel agents.

**Domain name:** unique Internet address used to identify a Website, e.g. www.futurefilter.com

**e-business:** using the Internet or other electronic means to conduct business. The two most common models are B2C (Business-to-Consumer) and B2B (Business-to-Business). Partly due to news coverage given to high profile companies like Amazon, B2C is the better known model; on the other hand, B2B is growing faster than its more glamorous cousin.

**e- by gum:** a term to describe the quaint practice of sending a message via the traditional postal service using a sealed envelope.

**e-commerce:** commercial activity conducted via the Internet.

**Ego surfing:** looking on the Web for occurrences of one's own name.

**e-lancers:** independent contractors connected through personal computers and electronic networks. These electronically connected freelancers – e-lancers – join together into fluid and temporary networks to produce and sell goods and services.

**e-tailing:** a retail strategy based on selling and order processing via the Web.

**e-zines:** the online equivalent of print-based newsletters and magazines.

**Eyeballs:** a measure of the number of visits made to a Website.

**Globalization:** the integration of economic activity across national or regional boundaries, a process that is being accelerated by the impact of information technology.

**Going dot.com:** the trend that started in the US of leaving a well-paid job to join an Internet organization.

**Head-shunting:** a term that describes when employers suggest to headhunters that they should contact a capable but troublesome employee. Companies occasionally pay a discreet fee to the headhunter, reckoning that to be cheaper than the cost of an exit package or an industrial tribunal.

**HTML:** abbreviation for Hypertext Markup Language, a computer language, the one that most Web pages are currently written in.

**Infomediary:** a business wherein the primary source of revenue derives from capturing customer information and developing detailed profiles of individual consumers for use by selected third-party vendors. In other words, an infomediary is a company or individual that makes money by bridging the gap between companies' need for capture of detailed customer information and customers' desire for protection of such information from exploitation by companies.

**Informate:** to apply technology to translate and make visible – processes, objects, behaviors, and events are translated into data and made visible by the display of those data.
Source: Shoshana Zuboff (1988) *In the Age of the Smart Machine*, Basic Books, USA.

**Intellectual capital:** intellectual material – knowledge, information, intellectual property, experience – that can be put to use to create wealth. In a business context, the sum total of what employees in an organization know that gives it a competitive edge.

**The Internot:** business executives or organizations that see no value from getting online. The term was devised by psychologist David Lewis, who also coined the phrase "road rage" to describe when motoring frustration spills over. Research conducted by Lewis suggests that about half of all managers are Internots.

**Intranet:** a network designed to organize and share information that is accessible only by a specified group or organization.

**ISP:** abbreviation for Internet Service Provider, the party that connects users to the Internet.

**Killer app:** a new good or service that establishes an entirely new category and, by being first, dominates it, returning several hundred percent on the initial investment.
Source: Larry Downes and Chunka Mui (1998) *Unleashing the Killer App*, Harvard Business School Press, USA

**Knowledge management:** a system, most often computer-based, to share information in a company with the goal of increasing levels of responsiveness and innovation.

**LOPSOD:** Long On Promises, Short On Delivery – a much-hyped product whose performance disappoints.

**Mass customization:** the cost-efficient mass production as a matter of routine of goods and services in lot sizes of one or just a few at a time.

Source: Don Peppers and Martha Rogers (1997) *Enterprise One-to-One*, Doubleday, USA.

**m-commerce:** David Potter, Chairman of Psion, predicts that electronic commerce, today conducted largely via Internet connected desk-tops will soon be overtaken by mobile (or m-) commerce using mobile phone technology.

**Meme:** an idea, behavior, or skill that can be transferred from one person to another by imitation. Examples include the way in which we copy ideas, inventions, songs, catch-phrases and stories from one another. In a wired global economy, memes will have the capability of spreading at astonishing speeds.

Source: Richard Dawkins (1978) *The Selfish Gene*, Oxford University Press, UK

**Microissues:** the questions that matter most, both to the people living within a macro-culture and to an external understanding of the people and their epoch.

Source: Watts Wacker and Jim Taylor (2000) *The Visionary's Handbook*, HarperBusiness, USA

**Netiquette:** a system of tacit codes encouraging members of the on-line community to uphold certain standards of behavior.

**Net generation:** the first generation to grow up surrounded by digital media. Tapscott: "the youngest of these kids are still in diapers and the eldest are just turning twenty."

Source: Don Tapscott (1998) *Growing up Digital*, McGraw-Hill, USA

**New capitalism:** "Old capitalism's giant companies had vast numbers of employees; new capitalism's giant companies have few employees. The issues of old capitalism – law on property, contract, limited liability, tort, bankruptcy – all of these are no longer really appropriate. The key assets of new capitalism are not defined as physical property but as intellectual assets, many embedded in people."

From an interview with Robert Reich, former US Secretary for Labor, published in *New Statesman*, November 14, 1997

**One-to-one marketing:** customizing and personalizing a product or service to meet an individual's specific needs.

**Out of the garage:** a term for a young company that has just moved to its first real office.

**Portal:** Web page that serves as a start-point or central directory for a range of Internet services.

**Portfolio working:** a work portfolio is a way of describing how the different bits of work in our life fit together to form a balanced whole. There are five main categories of work for the portfolio: *wage work* and *fee work*, which are both forms of paid work; *homework*, *gift work* and *study work*, which are all free work.

Source: Charles Handy (1989) *The Age of Unreason*, Hutchinson, UK

**Product overlap:** this occurs when more than one generation of the same product is available simultaneously. The original version of a piece of software may sell at a reduced price alongside the latest version at a higher price.

**Prospect theory:** according to this theory, people are more motivated by their losses than their gains and this results in increasingly risky behavior as losses accumulate. For example, long-odds bets are more popular in the last horse race of the day than the first. By the end of the day, punters have lost most of their gambling money and hope to win it all back with a single long-shot bet that they would not have considered taking in the first race.

**Push technology:** the delivery of news and multimedia information via the World Wide Web to personal computers on people's desks. The Web is basically a "pull" medium. Users decide what they want, point their browsers at the relevant Website and then pull the designated pages back to their PCs.

**Re-purposing:** originally coined by US TV executives to describe the process of "freshening up" a new series of a well established TV series whose popularity is flagging by introducing new characters and plot-lines. The term is now being adopted by companies seeking to re-establish forward momentum.

**Scenario fixations:** believing that one thing is happening when the reality is completely different. In 1988, the warship USS Vincennes was involved with potentially hostile Iranian vessels. A series of rapid maneuvers added to the tension and in the general confusion, the crew incorrectly identified a civilian Airbus 320 as an Iranian F14 fighter, then misheard its identification signals, and mistakenly thought that it was descending towards the ship when it was in fact on its usual flight path. The warship fired two missiles at the airliner, killing all 290 passengers. The ship's computer system had performed perfectly throughout.

**Silver surfers:** a term used to denote older members of the population who are comfortable "surfing" the Internet for information and services.

**Spam:** in a phrase, junk e-mail – unwanted messages sent to uninterested recipients.

**Spendorphins:** the pleasure proteins that seem to be released during a shopping frenzy.

**Sticky content:** the term refers to whether a Website is alluring enough to "catch" visitors as they go flying past. Until recently, most companies have concentrated their Website efforts on increasing the flow of traffic to their site. Companies are now realizing that the emphasis needs to be less on attracting visitors on a one-off basis, and more on enticing visitors to stay, return again and even tell their friends.

**Strategic inflection points:** a moment in the life of a business when its fundamentals are about to change for better or worse.

Source: Andy Grove (1996) *Only the Paranoid Survive*, HarperBusiness, USA

**3Cs:** champagne, caviar and Concorde – the alleged extravagant lifestyle that in May 2000 helped high-profile boo.com become the first UK Internet stock to go to the wall.

**10X force:** a super-competitive force that threatens the future of a business.

Source: Andy Grove (1996) *Only the Paranoid Survive*, HarperBusiness, USA

**Technology adoption life cycle:** model created by Geoffrey A. Moore to demonstrate the various points at which individuals will become involved with a technological innovation. Moore identifies five key groups that will become involved with any new technology at various stages of its life cycle:

1 Innovators: the technology enthusiasts.
2 Early adopters: the visionaries.
3 Early majority: the pragmatists.
4 Late majority: the conservatives.
5 Laggards: the skeptics.

**Viral marketing:** releasing a catchy message, typically using online, with a view to the message reaching growing numbers of people, initially organically but then exponentially.

**Virtual organization:** an organizational form representing a loose combination of technology, expertise and networks.

**World Wide Web:** the set of all information accessible using computers and networking.

**Xanadu:** computer scientist Ted Nelson's planned global hypertext project, generally recognized as a forerunner of the Web.

**Zombies:** dot.com companies that are on their last legs, waiting for their cash-burn rate to kill off the business.

# About the Author

J ohn Middleton is the founder of the Bristol Management Research Centre. He also edits and publishes *Future Filter*, a bi-monthly business digest for the new economy.

Recognized as a visionary and quirky business thinker, he works extensively with organizations (consultancy stuff) and individuals (coaching stuff) who are trying to make best sense of the future.

*Writing the New Economy* is his first book. He is currently working on his second (and third).

He can be contacted at john@futurefilter.com
www.futurefilter.com

# Index